Wakefield Libraries
& Information Services

This book should be returned by the last date stamped
above. You may renew the loan personally, by post or
telephone for a further period if the book is not required by
another reader.

For Hugo

FMacD

Published in Great Britain in MMXIII by
Book House, an imprint of
The Salariya Book Company Ltd
25 Marlborough Place, Brighton BN1 1UB

Visit
www.salariya.com
for our online catalogue and
free interactive web books.

CATS

A very peculiar history™

Fiona Macdonald

Created and designed by
David Salariya

66

Strange it is this
speechless thing,
Subject to our mastering,
Subject for his life and food
To our gift, and time, and
mood…

Thomas Hardy (1840–1928),
'Last Words to a Dumb Friend'

99

Contents

"

There are no ordinary cats.

Sidonie-Gabrielle Colette (1873–1954)

"

INTRODUCTION

Loved and cherished, praised and admired, hated and feared. More than any other domesticated creature, cats provoke extremes of feeling.

Cats are contradictory.

Cats are the world's most popular pet. Given the independent, elusive nature of the beast and the lack of compulsory cat registration schemes, precise figures are hard to come by. But estimates suggest that there are well over 220 million cats-with-owners, and maybe twice as many feral or semi-feral cats worldwide. That's almost 660 million! In 2006, cat expert Dr David Sands calculated that worldwide there was one cat for every 34 people, although national ratios vary. According to the American Humane Society, one in every three United States households has a cat – or, more likely, two. In the United Kingdom, there is one cat for every ten people; in Austria, the cat and human populations are – staggeringly – just about equal!

However, cats are also the most likely domestic creature to provoke dismay ('Those poor wee mice! That beautiful bird!'), disgust ('Oh no! Why won't it use a litter tray?!') and even violent persecution ('Lousy little killing machines! Better off dead!'). More rationally, cats give rise to major environmental concerns in many parts of the world, and can spread serious diseases. Rabies and toxoplasmosis are probably the most dangerous. And, of course, cats harbour worms and fleas. They are on the official IUCN (International Union for the Conservation of Nature) list of the worlds' 100 most dangerous and destructive species.

Them and us

We humans have a strange habit of loading other creatures with values and attributes that more properly belong to us, as thinking, reasoning creatures, all alone. We call dogs faithful, horses brave and monkeys mischievous.

Following this pattern, cats' natural behaviour has been interpreted in an astonishing variety of ways. It has inspired paintings, stories, poems, proverbs, cartoons, films – even music.

Cats have been used as symbols of everything from black magic and savage promiscuity to heavenly beauty or the cosiest, most innocent domesticity. They have been seen as scapegoats, moral exemplars, channels of divine and human benevolence. They have been called bloodstained and disgusting, refined and spiritual, faithful and fickle, cruel and self-seeking, electric, sensual, gentle and loving – sometimes, all at once.

Les Chats

Passionate lovers and dry-as-dust scholars
Both befriend cats in their riper years.
Cats powerful and gentle, proud, domestic,
Like them, are stay-at-homes and feel the cold.

Friends of knowledge and of sensual pleasure,
They seek the silent horrors of the dark.
If their pride would allow them to obey orders
They would pull the funeral carts of hell.

Dozing, they assume the noble pose
Of great sphinxes, stretched across
  unfathomable solitudes,
Who seem to sleep in a dream without end;

Their loins spark magical fertility
And flecks of gold, as of the finest sand,
Gleam star-like in their mysterious eyes.

Charles Baudelaire, *Les Chats* (*The Cats*), 1847
(author's translation)

So what's the big attraction? Why do so many millions of us like cats? How, when, where, and for what reasons have we humans loaded a small, sleek, soft, subtle, scratchy, smelly carnivore with such a vast weight of meaning? Read on, and find out more.

A home without a cat, and a well-fed, well-petted, and a properly revered cat, may be a perfect home, perhaps, but how can it prove its title?

Mark Twain, *Pudd'nhead Wilson*, 1894

"

The modern domestic cat is
the product of 11 million
years of natural selection in
a world free of people...

Carlos A. Driscoll, David W. Macdonald and
Stephen J. O'Brian, *Procedings of the National
Academy of Sciences of the USA*, 2009

"

CHAPTER ONE

HOW THE CAT BECAME...

The Death of the Dinosaurs: an awesome extinction! A bonanza event for future fossil hunters, an inspiration for blockbuster movie-makers, and part of probably the greatest ecological upheaval the world has ever seen. Although scientists do not all agree as to what caused the cataclysm, most seem confident that around two-thirds of all plant and animal species living on planet Earth died out around 65.5 million years ago. Including the dinosaurs – but not cats.

This side of the KT horizon (geologists' name for the boundary between the Cretaceous Era, when dinosaurs roamed, and the subsequent Tertiary Era, when they did not) was a strange – and relatively empty – new world. Because, when the dinosaurs died, they left behind a space for a dominant animal. Who or what could replace them as the most powerful life-form on the planet?

Not birds (close dinosaur relatives, who survived, but in miniature). Not insects, or bacteria, or corals or fishes, or forest trees (although they survived, as well). Step forward the mammals! Warm-blooded creatures that suckled and cared for their young. Mammals already came in many shapes and sizes – big, small, fat, thin…

Now, hold tight for a rather bumpy ride through a forest of strange names. For a creature known almost all round the world by a single short, sharp syllable (see page 97), the cat has some grand-sounding ancestors.

Cat ancestors

They begin with the **Miacids**: small carnivores, looking something like a modern weasel, with sandy-brown spotted fur and long, stripy, bushy tails. They ate insects and then chose more meaty prey: lizards, birds and smaller mammals. They had sharp teeth and claws; they could climb trees. Their patterned coats were excellent camouflage amid leaves and branches.

The Miacid family survived for around 29 million years, and they are the very, very, very far distant ancestors of all modern carnivores: bears, seals, dogs – and, of course, cats, big and small.

The cats' ancestory is complex, but the simplified diagram overleaf shows the gist of it.

Cats: A Very Peculiar History

Cat family tree

Carnivora

Felidae

Canidae (dog family)

Leopardis

Panthera

Felis

Lynx

Puma

Ocelot

Bobcat

Cheetah

Cougar

Tiger

Leopard

Lion

Jaguar

Jungle cat

African wildcat

European wild cat

Domestic cat

Breaking away

However, by around 53 million years ago, one group of Miacids had left dogs and bears behind, to occupy a different ecological niche. Slowly, the breakaways evolved into new creatures: the **Feloidea**. They were the ancestors of all cats living today (and of some extinct catlike creatures); they had long legs and a long tail, and sharp, catlike fangs. However, the first 'true' cat – *Proailurus* – did not evolve from its ancestors until around 30 million years ago.

Proailurus was bigger than the early Miacids. It had more teeth, especially well adapted for tearing meat. Its big eyes helped it see in the dark as well as in daylight, and its long tail helped it balance when climbing high. Like modern cats, it could land safely on its feet if it fell.

Proailurus also had claws that could be retracted (drawn in) when not in use – a great evolutionary improvement. This meant that each claw's sharp point was protected if *Proailurus* chose to descend from the trees and hunt on the forest floor. But the claws could still be stretched out at will if it wanted to climb trees or grab hold of its prey.

Still, early cats went on evolving, growing more and more specialised over the years. Slowly, they became what modern scientists call 'obligate carnivores'; creatures with a very limited ability to metabolise any foodstuff except protein. They spread across Europe, Africa and Asia, and from there to America, across the Bering Strait land bridge (the seabed between far-eastern Russia and Alaska, uncovered when the world's seas froze during past Ice Ages.) There were also catlike creatures in Australia, but they were rather different…

Q: When is a lion not a big cat?

A: When it's related to a wombat!

Thylacoleonidae were lion-like marsupials (animals with pouches) that lived in Australia about 100 million years ago. They evolved from ancient plant-eating creatures; their nearest living relatives are wombats and koalas. They ranged from the size of a modern house-cat to a lion, and were among the most highly specialised killers and meat-eaters ever to live on this planet. They had huge carnassial (cheek) teeth and strong, sharp incisors (front teeth), plus claws as sharp as knives on their front paws.

From ancient to modern

By about 20 million years ago, *Proailurus* had evolved into first, *Silvaeurus*, and then a much larger creature, *Pseudaelurus*, with longer legs than its ancestors. In turn, *Pseudaelurus* changed and adapted, breaking away from their close relatives: the **Machairodontinae**: cats with long, flat and fearsome sabre-teeth; all are now extinct – probably.

Time passes, nothing stays the same – least of all, living creatures. Facing constant pressure to adapt and survive, some time around 18 million years ago, *Pseudaelurus* evolved into the first recognisable **Felidae** (true cats). These were fast, sleek, long-legged and round-headed. Modern cheetahs, *Acinonyx*, descended from them around 7.2 million years ago.

It took another 6 million years before *Felis*, the earliest small cats, appeared on our planet, around 12 million years ago. *Felis* hunted by stalking or ambushing, instead of chasing prey like cheetahs. They killed by biting (usually at the back of the neck) and the shape of their throats gave them a special ability – to purr.

These little cats spread throughout Europe, Asia and Africa, adapting their appearance, body type and behaviour to different environments, from snowy mountain slopes to hot deserts and grasslands. Today, scientists list 10 different members of the modern *Felis* species:

- Manul, or Pallas's cat
- Serval
- Asian and African golden cats (and others)
- Leopard cat, fishing cat (and others)
- Pampas cat
- Ocelot, marguay (and others)
- Andean mountain cat
- Jaguarundi
- Cougar
- and, last but not least, the modern wildcat (*Felis sylvestris sylvestris*) and its close relative, the domestic cat.

The last group – and the largest in size – of the modern cats to evolve were *Panthera*, lions and tigers, around 3 million years ago. They typically killed by biting the necks of their victims and suffocating them, and they roared rather than purred.

How Scientists classify cats today

Kingdom Animalia *Animals*

Phylum Chordata *Animals with spinal cords*

Class Mammalia *Animals that suckle young*

Order Carnivora *Animals that eat meat*

Superfamily Aeluroidea *Cats, hyenas, mongooses etc.*

Family Felidae *Modern cats*

Subfamily
Machairodontinae
Sabretoothed cats (extinct)

Subfamily
Acinonychinae
Cheetahs

Subfamily
Pantherinae
Tiger, lion etc.

Subfamily
Felinae
Small cats (including the modern domestic cat)

Wildcats worldwide

Many early *Felis* (purring) cats did not survive – including *Felis lunensis*, a small, stocky cat with a wonderful striped tail that lived in Europe around 10 million years ago. But by about 2 million years ago, its descendant *Felis sylvestris* (woodland cat) had evolved most successfully to live and hunt among European trees and forests. It had a thick, dense coat, camouflaged by stripes and brindled fur; it enjoyed good night vision and excellent hearing. It was a fierce hunter; shy, cautious, with rapid reactions and brief bursts of speed (up to 30 mph/48 kph, for a while). It was strong and brave (it could fight prey its own size), and a great survivor. So much so, that it is still with us today. Its most famous modern representative is probably the wonderful Scottish wildcat (*Felis sylvestris sylvestris*), but, as we shall see, that has many wildcat relatives, worldwide.

Over the centuries, early *Felis sylvestris* wildcats spread south, to Asia and Africa. During the Ice Ages, when glaciers covered the earth, wildcats had to leave Europe altogether, although when the ice melted, they soon returned. In new, warmer, drier, habitats, *Felis sylvestris* continued to evolve into many separate wildcat subspecies. For example, Asian and African wildcats are slimmer and less bulky than their north European relatives; their coats are thinner, and their ears larger and less hairy. Their kidneys are so efficient that some of them can survive without drinking much for days at a time (they get all the moisture they need from prey). They can cope with very high temperatures – over 50°C – if they have shade and water. Today, scientists recognise five main subspecies of *Felis sylvestris* (plus several local variations):

- Europe: *Felis sylvestris silvestris*
  (big, thickset, striped tabbies)

- South Africa: *Felis sylvestris cafra*

- Central Asia: *Felis sylvestris ornata*

- Tibet/China: *Felis sylvestris bieti*
  (these three subspecies are small, slim;
  with long, pointed tails and buff speckled fur)

- Near East: *Felis sylvestris lybica*
  (small, slim, pale fur with spots and bands)

All five of these wildcat subspecies are genetically close to each other. They are also related to today's pet cats, which are, scientifically speaking, yet another subspecies: *Felis sylvestris catus*. But genetic studies have shown that only one kind of wildcat is the ancestor of all our modern moggies, wherever they live and whatever they look like.

So where do our present-day furry friends come from? How did they get from mountain, forest, desert or grassland into our homes? And what made wildcats change from shy, wild creatures to confident, sometimes extremely demanding companions? We'll address this question in Chapter 4, but in the meantime...

"

It is a Beast of prey…it being in the opinion of many nothing but a diminutive Lyon…

It has a broad Face… short Ears, large Whiskers, shining Eyes, short smooth Hair, long Tail, rough Tongue, and armed on its Feet with Claws…

William Salmon, Alchemist and quack doctor, 1644–1713

CHAPTER TWO

A DIMINUTIVE
LYON

They called him 'The Furry Grim Reaper'. In 2007, a grey and white cat named Oscar hit the headlines, when doctors at the nursing home where he was a pet, in Rhode Island, USA, announced that he was better than they were at spotting which patients were about to die. In 25 well-documented cases, Oscar – who normally kept his distance from sick people – had gone to sit on the bed of a seriously ill man or woman. Then, usually within about 4 hours, that person had passed away.

How did Oscar do it? Was he psychic? Spooky? Linked by a hotline to heaven? Possibly, he was attracted by the warmth of each death-bed; nurses often kept gravely ill patients comfortable with heating pads. But the most likely explanation, according to the doctors, was that Oscar was making use of his phenomenal sense of smell. They believed that Oscar's nose could detect minute biochemical changes that occur in the human body shortly before death. Presumably, Oscar was attracted to their scent.

Oscar's nose may have been exceptionally acute. But even an average cat has between 12 and 20 times more 'smelling capacity' than a human, if we compare the number of olfactory cells in each species. Cats have between 60 and 80 million receptors sensitive to airborne substances in their noses (some experts say up to 200 million); humans have between five and twenty million.

An ability to detect extremely faint smells is just one feature of the cat's highly evolved and very specialised anatomy. Let's take a quick tour of the beast, from nose to tail, to look at a few of the marvels concealed beneath the fur of even the most ordinary moggy.

Bigger and better?

The average domestic cat weighs between 4 and 5 kilograms. A few breeds, especially huge, hefty Maine Coon cats bred in the northeast of the U.S., can weigh twice as much or even more.

The world's heaviest known domestic cat was a Siamese, from Russia. In 2003, it was reported to tip the scales at 50 lb (23 kg). Its closest rival was Himmie, a tabby cat from Australia, that was said to weigh almost 46 lb (21 kg). Poor Himmie was too fat to walk far – he was moved around in a wheelbarrow – and may have suffered from a medical condition that made him put on weight uncontrollably. No-one accused his owners of ill-treatment, but vets and animal lovers suspected that other unscrupulous pet-owners were deliberately overfeeding their cats to win a place in the record books, and so the search for the 'world's fattest cat' was discontinued.

At the opposite end of the spectrum, the world's lightest known adult cat, a brown tabby named Mr Peebles, weighed a mere 3.3 lb/1.5 kg in 2007. He was about the same size as a guinea pig. Almost inevitably, Britain's *The Sun* newspaper (famous for its catchy headlines) labelled him an 'itty-bitty-kitty'.

An average male cat stands around 25 cm high at the shoulder, and measures around 46 cm from nose to base of tail. Females are usually slightly smaller. According to the *Guinness Book of Records*, the longest known cat is a Maine Coon measuring 122 cm; Mr Peebles (above) was the shortest in height, measuring only 15.5 cm to his shoulders.

A long life…

With luck, good care and attention – and not too much traffic nearby (traffic accidents are the leading cause of untimely death among pet cats) – a domestic cat can hope to live to around 14 years old. Unless he is an entire (un-neutered) tomcat, with the freedom to range far and wide, in which case he'll be lucky to live much longer than four or five years. The oldest known cat was Crème Puff, who celebrated her 38th birthday in 2004.

Whisker, whisker

One of the cat family's most instantly recognisable features, these moveable, thickened bristles, more than twice the diameter of ordinary hairs, taper sharply towards the tips. An average cat has 24 main whiskers, arranged in rows of four on either side of its nose, plus lesser whiskers on its cheeks, above its eyes, and at the back of its front legs. The thickest end of each whisker is embedded in the skin to three times the depth of ordinary hairs, and is connected to a cluster of nerve-endings that carry supersensitive messages to the cat's brain.

Cats use their whiskers to signal emotions, to judge distance – can they squeeze through that cat flap? – and also, most importantly, to navigate, especially in the dark. Whiskers can sense minute air currents stirred up when a cat moves past a solid object, or when a mouse quivers with fear. A blindfolded cat can use its whiskers to make its way around a crowded room; a cat with damaged whiskers finds it difficult to hunt – or go anywhere unfamiliar – at night.

Nose to nose

Each cat's nose makes a separate, unique pattern, similar to fingerprints in humans. More importantly, as in the case of Oscar (above), cats' noses can distinguish scents that are undetectable to humans. When a cat sniffs, scent molecules land on olfactory receptors that cover an amazing area of 40 square cm (6 square inches) in the damp lining of its nose, triggering reactions of recognition, pleasure or fear in the brain.

Smell is probably the sense that is most important to cats, and the most commonly utilised. Cats use odours to investigate, identify, accept or reject food, friends, enemies and safe places. They depend on their ability to recognise and 'understand' smells for survival. Newborn kittens – which cannot see

– locate their mother, and her milk, entirely by smell; old cats lose their appetite and may waste away as their sense of smell diminishes. Cats also mark their owners and their territories with their own individual scents. But more of that below on pages 44–45.

Just like dogs, humans, and many other creatures, a cat's sense of smell is closely linked to its sense of taste. But cats also have a third sense, halfway between the two. This is operated by the vomeronasal – or Jacobson's – organ in the roof of a cat's mouth, at the back. Cats use their tongues to flick scented molecules onto this sensor, which passes signals to the brain rather as if they were smells. As they do this, cats half-open their mouths in a very strange expression: the Flehmen reaction. It is also shown when cats sniff catnip.

Catnip trip

Catnip or catmint (*Nepeta cataria*) is a herb that grows wild in Europe and North America. It contains a scented chemical (nepetalactone) that provokes extreme reactions in some cats, although others seem completely indifferent. A second, unrelated, herb, valerian, has a similar effect.

Susceptible cats, whatever their gender, can detect nepetalactone at dilutions of one part per billion. And then they display behaviour rather like an adult female during the mating season. They snuffle, roll over, rub themselves against people or furniture, and yowl with wild abandon. They may seem to chase invisible prey or stare blankly into space.

Scientists say that the areas of the cat's brain affected by catmint or valerian are similar to those stimulated in humans who ingest LSD or other hallucinogenic drugs. But unlike humans, cats seem to suffer no long-lasting ill effects from their trips.

Lick and lap

Long, strong and very flexible, a cat's tongue has several separate functions. It is used to drink liquids, for washing, to display affection or dominance (to other cats and humans), and, of course, for tasting. Unlike many other mammals, cats do not have a sweet tooth; their taste buds – arranged around the edges of the tongue – are more sensitive to bitter, salty or acid flavours. Cats are, however, extremely aware of the taste of water. Many cat owners have watched, puzzled, as pussy laps raindrops from a dirty puddle, or even climbs into the lavatory for a drink, but ignores the nice clean, chemically treated, tap water in its bowl in the kitchen. When drinking, a cat curves its tongue into a spoon shape, and laps at the rate of four flicks of the tongue per second – too fast for the human eye to see. It swallows after every four or five laps.

Cats' taste buds are also able to detect fine differences between the flavours of various meats – from mice and birds to tinned cat food. Given a choice, many cats will show strong preferences. It is a myth that all cats love fish, but it is true that they prefer food warm (at tongue temperature, 86°F/30°C) rather than chilled, from the refrigerator.

The centre of a cat's tongue is not used at all for tasting. Instead, it is covered in rough, round, backward-facing hooks, called *papillae*. Like sandpaper, these help to rasp raw flesh from bones. Or else they hold food – especially if it is still alive and struggling. They also act as brushes when the cat grooms itself.

Once bitten…

A cat is an extremely efficient killing machine, and the main tools it uses to catch and dispatch its prey are its long, sharp teeth. Adult cats have 30 teeth; two fewer than humans. They cannot chew, but use their teeth to cut, crunch or crush their food into small enough pieces for swallowing.

• **4 canines** (2 upper, 2 lower) = fangs, used for biting – typically at the back of the neck to sever the victim's spinal cord. Also used to hold and tear flesh.

- **12 incisors** (6 upper, 6 lower) = tiny rippers and scrapers.
- **10 premolars** (6 upper, 4 lower) = curved, pointed blades.
- **4 molars** (2 upper, 2 lower) = back teeth, also blade-shaped. The molars and premolars ('carnassials') work together like shears.

Shining bright

Beautiful, enigmatic – what *is* that cat thinking? – and shining, shining bright, cat's eyes are truly remarkable. They are especially well adapted for hunting, being large, forward-facing in the head, with a short focal length and a wide field of vision, plus binocular focus. They provide the cat with excellent 3-D vision, so that it can locate and follow moving prey with great accuracy. A cat sees best things that are 2–6 metres (7–20 ft) away.

Famously, cats' eyes also work very well in the dark: their pupils quickly adjust to varying light levels, from narrow slits in bright light to wide circles at nighttime. This allows the maximum amount of available light to strike the retina (layer of light-sensitive cells) at the back of the eyeball. A special mirror-like structure, the *tapetum lucidum*, sits behind the retina to reflect back any light that the retina did not absorb straight away. Together, the extra-sensitive retina plus the tapetum lucidum mean that a cat's nighttime vision is six times better than a human's. A cat's eye is, however, much less sensitive to colour. Cats mostly see in (goodness knows how many) shades of grey, plus some blue and some green.

Supersonic!

That's the only word – although, strictly, it's not quite accurate. Cats' ears can hear most of the same sounds as humans, but they can also detect sound waves at a pitch – 65 kHz or more – almost three octaves higher than the limit of human hearing. This helps them when hunting; their natural prey squeaks or chirps. It may also explain why some cats seem to respond more to women's or children's voices. Cats are far more sensitive to faint sounds than humans; they move the large pinnae (outer flaps) of their ears independently from each other to detect the direction of a sound or to catch and amplify a distant rustle or murmur.

Engineering excellence

For such small creatures, cats have a marvellously intricate structure. A cat's skeleton contains around 240 bones; a human's, although much larger, contains only 206. Cats' tails vary in length, containing from 18 to 28 vertebrae (spinal bones). A cat's spine is much more flexible than any other mammal's. It can arch its back into a complete 'U' shape, curl round into a tight ball, and twist the front part of its body through 180 degrees.

Attached to these cat bones are around 500 muscles – the largest are in the back legs. All give a cat great strength and agility. An average cat can jump five times its own height, and climb much higher. Cats also walk and run with extraordinary control, grace and precision. Even big, heavy cats can move silently, or make their way along a narrow plank. Cats' movements are co-ordinated by an area of the brain known as the cerebellum. Their narrow chests and long tails increase their balancing abilities.

Making tracks

Cats stand on the tips of their toes, with the other bones in their feet making up the lower portion of each leg. At a slow walking pace, they move two legs on one side of the body and then two legs on the other side. They usually place each hind paw almost directly in the print made by the front one. This minimises the sound they make, and the tracks they leave behind them. However, when running, cats' legs move diagonally; front legs and back legs on opposite sides of the body move together, in turn.

Q: Why do cats get stuck up trees?

1. Because climbing is fun?
2. Because cats are chased by dogs or other enemies?
3. Because cats don't know when to stop while hunting?
4. Because cats' claws grip much better when going up?
5. Because cats are stupid?
6. Because cats get scared?
7. Because cats can't climb down head first?
8. Because sliding down backwards is dangerous and undignified?

A: All answers are correct, except no 5.

Falling on its feet

Cats are proverbially famous for being able to turn their bodies round as they fall, and land on all fours. How can they do this?

• Cats have an acute sense of balance, maintained by a series of organs (the vestibular apparatus) in the inner ear. This lets a cat know, all the time, which way up it is.

• As we have seen, they have strong muscles and a very flexible spine.

• A cat's collarbones are very small or non-existent. Its front legs are attached to the shoulder bone by muscles. This helps a cat run faster and squeeze into narrow spaces. The muscles also absorb shock when a cat lands.

• Cats have a 'righting reflex'. When falling, they first turn their heads the right way up, as dictated by their sense of balance. Then they bring their front paws close to their head, and twist their back limbs round until their whole body is parallel with the ground. They use their tail to steady their spine, so they do not twist too far. Finally, they extend their legs and arch their backs, ready to land.

A cat can perform this lifesaving acrobatic manoeuvre from as little as 1 m (3 ft) from the ground. Competing claims have been made about the longest fall that a cat has survived; but in 2012, cat Sugar from Boston, USA walked away almost unharmed – apart from a chipped tooth – after falling almost 60 m (200 ft) from an apartment window.

Pins and needles

Claws! Oh, how destructive! The bane of so many cat-lovers' lives. Why will kitty scratch the walls, the carpets, the sofa, instead of the trees and fence-posts outside? To combat this annoying behaviour, some pet owners in the past had their cats de-clawed. Today animal welfare organisations, and many vets, consider this cruel and unacceptable.

Unlike most other species, cats have retractable claws. Each claw – a sharp, pointed, toughened fingernail – is attached to the distal (end) toe-bone, which is in turn attached to neighbouring bones and muscles by stretchy ligaments and tendons. When the muscles contract, the toe-bone is pushed forward and the claw appears.

Cats can sheathe their claws at will, one paw at a time. This protects the claws' sharp tips, and helps the cat move silently. Cats choose to extend their claws for hunting, fighting, getting extra grip on slippery ground, when washing – or to mark their territory. When a cat scratches a surface, scent glands close to its paw pads leave a smelly 'signature'. Kitty doesn't aim to leave scratch marks or destroy your upholstery. She's just telling the world that this is her home.

A game of cat and mouse?

Cats are carnivores, red in tooth and claw. They need to eat meat. But sometimes it seems as if they also take a sadistic delight in killing. How often has a kind-hearted cat owner wished that their pet would just kill its prey cleanly, instead of patting and pawing and pouncing and clawing, prolonging the poor victim's misery?

Why do cats play with their prey? There are two possible reasons; both may be true. Firstly, a cat has to make very, very sure that any creature it has caught is too weak to fight back before delivering the final killing bite – typically, to the nape of the neck. Secondly, a successful hunt is tremendously exciting. Some cats just get carried away, repeating the catching sequence over and over again.

Ten little tiny fingers?

No. Normal cats have five toes on each front paw, and four on each hind paw. But a mutant gene, common along the eastern seaboard of America and in the southwest of Britain, produces a condition called polydactyly, where cats may have extra toes on one or all of their paws. This does not usually cause the cat any problems, and cats with extra toes have become favourite pets with some owners. In the past, sailors believed that they were lucky.

The most famous friend of polydactyl cats was United States writer Ernest Hemingway (died 1961). He kept a six-toed cat at his home in Florida. Today, Hemingway's home is a museum, and around 50 of his cat's descendants live there. Many have inherited the mutant gene.

Several different cats claim the record for the largest number of toes. One of the best known is Jake, from Canada. In 2012, he was confirmed as the proud possessor of 28 – ten more than any normal cat or kitten. In 2011, Daniel, a cat with

26 toes, featured in a fundraising campaign for an animal welfare shelter in Wisconsin, USA. Well-wishers were asked to donate $26 each, one dollar for each toe. An impressive sum was collected, and saved the shelter from the threat of closure.

To a Cat

I
Stately, kindly, lordly friend,
  Condescend
Here to sit by me, and turn
Glorious eyes that smile and burn,
Golden eyes, love's lustrous meed,
On the golden page I read.

All your wondrous wealth of hair,
  Dark and fair,
Silken-shaggy, soft and bright
As the clouds and beams of night,
Pays my reverent hand's caress
Back with friendlier gentleness...

Algernon Charles Swinburne (1837–1909), 'To a Cat'

Round and round

'Heartless' killers of mice though they may appear to be, cats – of course – have an efficient circulatory system, powered by heart and lungs. An adult cat's body contains almost half a pint (250 ml) of blood, and this takes about 11 seconds to flow round its body. A cat's heart beats almost twice as fast as a human's, at around 120–140 beats per minute. That's over 60 million beats per year. And, at up to 50 breaths (in and out) per minute when at rest, cats breathe almost four times as quickly as their owners.

In keeping with their fast pulse and breathing, cats also have a higher average body temperature than humans. In a healthy animal, it ranges from 100.5 to 102.5°F (38 to 39.2°C). Cats do not sweat, but, like dogs, pant to cool themselves. Unlike humans, cats' temperature remains much the same all day long, probably because they are active for short periods all around the clock, 24/7.

For I will consider
my Cat Jeoffry...

...First he looks upon his forepaws to
see if they are clean.
And secondly he kicks up behind to
clear away there.
And thirdly he works it upon stretch
with the forepaws extended.
For fourthly he sharpens his paws by
wood.
For fifthly he washes himself.
For sixthly he rolls upon wash.
For seventhly he fleas himself, that
he may not be interrupted upon the
beat.
For eighthly he rubs himself against a
post.
For ninthly he looks up for his
instructions.
For tenthly he goes in quest of
food...

Poet Christopher Smart, 'Jubilate Agno',
1759–1763

Last but not least, the mysterious feline brain

Oscar (see page 27) is not the only cat to have been credited with strange, extra-sensory powers. In the past, and sometimes still today, folk-tales, anecdotes, urban myths and newspaper reports, to say nothing of the wilder shores of the Internet, describe cats who seem intuitively to know when something nice (an owner returning home) or nasty (a planned trip to the vet) is about to happen.

Since ancient Roman times, people have claimed that animals can foretell approaching earthquakes, but in 2012, Japanese researchers linked to Kobe Zoo suggested that cats (and dogs) really could detect the electromagnetic waves that preceded major earth tremors. Cats are also sensitive to changes in barometric pressure, which precede severe storms.

There are tales of cats who trekked right across continents to return to their old homes. The most famous is probably Howie, handed over to trusted carers when his owners departed on an extended trip overseas. Howie and his owners lived in Adelaide, Australia; the carers (close relatives) had a home over 1,000 miles (1,609 km) away. Imagine their horror when, one day, Howie disappeared. Imagine Howie's owners' delight, when, one year later, he appeared, skinny, sickly, matted but still alive, at their front door.

By rather unhappily fixing strong magnets to cats' collars and observing their disorientation, scientists have shown that cats rely on a perception of the earth's magnetic forces to navigate. Howie's story – if true – shows just how effective this ability to 'read' magnetism can be.

Most feline exploits can be explained by reminding ourselves of cats' superhuman senses. And pets are usually much better, more patient, observers than humans. They notice subtle changes in body language or the smells given off by owners; they learn to expect routine patterns of behaviour. A bored or hungry cat is going to listen out for the sound of its owner's foot on the stair, and sit waiting as if it 'knew' food or company was approaching. In the same way, the slightest creak of the carrying basket will send many cats running for cover. Even so, a few cats' abilities are truly phenomenal:

Hero cat predicts epileptic fits

BBC News Channel, England, 2006

Black and white family pet Tee Cee has been praised for acting as 'a lifeline' to his owner, who suffers from a complex form of epilepsy. When Tee Cee senses that another seizure is coming, he sits on his owner's chest and stares at him, and then runs to attract the owner's wife's attention.

In 2006 Tee Cee was shortlisted for the Hero Cat title at the Rescue Cat of the Year awards, organised by the Cats' Protection animal welfare charity.

Canadian Cat Diagnoses Cancer

Now recovering from surgery to remove cancer from his lung, Adams, 59, is crediting his eight-year-old feline friend Tiger for alerting him and his family doctor... 'He would climb into bed and take his paw and drag it down my left side — he was adamant there was something there,' he [Adams] said. 'And it was right where the cancer was.'

Edmonton Sun, Canada, February 2009

Well, well, well.

Could Tiger smell chemicals produced by the tumour? Sense that his owner was breathing differently? Feel something suspicious under his paws? If only we could ask him!

"

On moonlit nights he roams
the woods or the roofs,
walking by his wild lone...

Rudyard Kipling,
The Cat that Walked by Himself, 1902

"

CHAPTER THREE

THE CAT THAT WALKED BY HIMSELF

The Vikings said that when a cat raised its back leg straight in the air behind its ear while washing, this was a sign that 'guest spears' were approaching. In other words, it was time to keep a look out, either for welcome visitors or for dangerous strangers!

The Vikings based their notion on close observation; when a cat lifts its back leg to wash, the four claws on its back paw are extended, like little spears.

How well can you read your pet? We may never know what thoughts or dreams dance behind those luminous eyes. But we can study cat behaviour, and learn to interpret typical cat gestures – although perhaps we might give them a rather different meaning from the warlike (and superstitious) Vikings. Read on for a quick guide to basic feline body language. But be warned, cats are great individualists, and some may decide to 'speak' in their own private or local dialects.

I see what you mean...

Cats have loud voices for their small size, and use them (see pages 64–65). But like almost all other animals, cats also use body language to send signals about their feelings or state of mind to other cats or to humans.

Face to face

Eyes, ears, whiskers, mouth, all play a part:

Eyes

• Eyes open, pupils normal (for prevailing light) = safe and happy

• Slit eyes = angry and stressed

- Wide-eyed, pupils dilated = frightened

- Open pupils, intense gaze = playing or hunting

- Eyes half-closed or blinking = pleased or being petted

- Eyes staring = intimidation or substitute fighting

- Third (horizontally-moving) eyelid showing = falling asleep or (if cat is awake) a sign of possible illness

They know, you know!

Q: Why do cats so often seem to make a bee-line for the only person in the room who does not like them?

A: Because that person is probably the only one who is not trying to make eye contact with them. Too much of that is threatening, especially from strangers. Cats will also turn their back to show that they are not interested, or as a way of avoiding potential conflict or contact with other cats and humans.

Whiskers

• Whiskers in relaxed, default position = cat happy

• Whiskers stiff, bristling, arched forward = angry and/or aggressive

• Whiskers flattened to face = frightened

• Whiskers forward and 'active' = hunting or playing

• Whiskers relaxed, maybe drooping = being petted

Mouth

• Mouth slightly open = hunting

• Mouth wide open, tongue flicking back = Flehmen reaction (see page 33): cat detecting very faint smells

• Lips curled back = angry or apprehensive

• Snarl, with fangs bared = ready to spring – look out!

• Licking self = normal grooming or a reaction to stress

• Licking others = a sign of affection or (when applied to other cats) a bid to dominate

Ears

- Perky, upright ears = all's well

- Ears upright but moved back = possible distaste

- Ears stiff and furled back = anger

- Ears flattened to head = frightened

- Ears upright and forward = playing or hunting

- Ears relaxed = pleased or being petted

Pleasure-seekers?

Q: Why do cats knead and sometimes drool – on their beds, the sofa, their owners?

A: Kneading is a way of seeking comfort, reassurance and pleasure. It's a throwback to kittenhood, when kneading a mother cat's abdomen stimulated the flow of milk for each kitten. Drooling and sucking wool – a problem if the cat swallows it – are probably for the same reasons.

Cats' tails

Tail

• Tail straight up in the air = friendly greeting (originally a kitten gesture when with a mother cat, so she can sniff, identify and wash as needed)

• End of tail flicking = anxious, undecided

• Whole tail twitching = irritated or scared

• Tail tip thumped fast up and down = very angry

• Tail held low and swished from side to side = suspicious and ready to attack

• Tail bent into inverted u-shape = advancing for attack

• Tail fluffed up = ready for defence

• Tail very low, stretched out or between legs = submissive or defeated

• Tail stretched backwards, with tip twitching = hunting or stalking

• Tail held high, back legs stiff and treading, a slight wiggle of the rear = OH NO! Another puddle!

Making a mark

Q: Why do male cats (and a few females) spray urine to mark their territory?

A: Because smell, even more than body-language, is cats' most important way of communicating. It is famously said that 'Dogs care about people; cats care about places.' Cats are territorial animals, and need to mark their home ground. It is also important for them to tell other nearby cats about their sex and status. Secretions from glands underneath the cat's tail add a pungent, long-lasting scent to feline urine.

As well as spraying, cats also mark their territories and their owners by rubbing against them. As they do this, scent glands on the cat's chin, forehead and tail leave individual signatures – clear to other cats, undetectable to most humans.

An ounce of civet?

In a famous scene from Shakespeare's tragedy *King Lear*, the deeply troubled hero asks for 'an ounce of civet' to 'sweeten his imagination'. Civet, a musky-smelling extract taken in Shakespeare's day from the perianal glands of beautiful spotted wild civet 'cats' (*Civettictis* or *Viverra civetta*, always called 'cats' but actually a member of the mongoose family), is one of the strongest-smelling and longest-lasting substances known to perfumers. An ounce of it might well have scented half of Lear's whole kingdom…

In Shakespeare's day, and until recently, perfumers obtained civet scent from hunters who trapped and killed civet cats, then cut out and preserved the relevant body parts. Just a tiny amount has a very powerful effect that was said to be alluring, and certainly made other scents last much longer.

Until 1998, civet was an ingredient in many famous perfumes, including allegedly 'Chanel No. 5', as reportedly worn by Marilyn Monroe.

Today animal civet is banned as an ingredient in perfumery and cosmetics. (This is one of several things animal-lovers can thank the so-called 'faceless European bureaucrats' for.) It has been replaced by a synthetic version of the same smell.

An extraordinary coffee is prepared in Vietnam and the Philippines. Wild coffee is eaten and partly digested by palm civet 'cats' (*Paradoxurus hermaphroditus*, a cousin of the perfume civets), and then excreted with the coffee seeds (beans) still intact. Civet faeces are collected, the coffee beans are extracted – and well washed, one hopes – and then roasted, ground and brewed into a drink, Kopi Luwak, that retails for up to US$100 per cup.

Meow, Meow

Cats don't talk, but do have a large vocabulary of sounds. Most are used to communicate with humans, rather than with other cats. Here are just some:

From kittens:
- Mew = Help! or I'm here!
- Wail = I'm lost or in danger!

From adult cats:
- Chirrup = Hello!
- High-pitched meow = It's me! or Pay attention!
- Low-pitched meow = I'm anxious or agitated.
- Meow ending on a rising tone = Please! or What on earth…!
- Snort! Sigh! = I'm getting impatient…
- Hiss! = I'm warning you! or Get off!
- Spit! = Look out! I've got claws and fangs!
- Wah-ah-ah = I'm a female cat who wants a mate. Come and get me!

• Muffled wow-wow-wow = My mouth is full but here is a lovely bird/mouse/lizard/bat I've brought you!

Duetto buffo di due Gatti (Humorous Duet for Two Cats),
a 19th-century pastiche incorporating music by
Rossini and others

One small purr for a cat

Q: Why do cats purr?

A: To show they are happy? To signal they need help? To say 'thank you'? To reduce pain? For all these reasons, and maybe more. A mother cat purrs to her kittens as she feeds them. The replying chorus of tiny whirrs and brrrs reassures her, and tells her that her brood is there and thriving.

There can be few happier sounds than a basket of nursing kittens, and many adult cats seem to preserve the memory. That is probably why they purr when their owners stroke them, or when they settle down on a nice, soft, cosy bed. But cats that are ill, or injured, or in distress, also purr frantically. Are they trying to soothe themselves, or asking their owner – or their mum – to comfort them and make them better?

Unlike humans (and lions and tigers), cats can purr when they breathe in as well as out. Even today, experts do not know exactly how.

Possibly, the purr is made as false vocal cords at the back of a cat's throat tremble in currents of air. Possibly it is made by vibrations as blood flows through a cat's chest cavity.

However, scientists at the University of California, USA, have made one startling discovery: continuous purring can help repair damaged bones and muscles. Sound waves produced by machines are already used by physiotherapists to treat injuries. It has seriously been suggested that the sound of purring cats might also stop bone density loss and muscle atrophy suffered by astronauts on space flights.

Aw, you shouldn't have bothered...

Q: Why do cats present their owners with 'gifts' of prey?

A: The experts say that it's because they are behaving like a mother cat, who brings prey to her kittens to show them how to hunt and kill. But even male cats bring these sad little presents to their owners, and adult cats don't normally share prey with each other. So – to this author at least – the habit remains a bit of a puzzle. And (N.B. cat Hamish, please) she really would have preferred NOT to have been offered a live and flapping bat in the bedroom at 2.00 a.m. the other morning...

Just so?

The Cat that Walked by Himself is one of Rudyard Kipling's (1865–1936) best-loved tales. First appearing in *The Ladies' Home Journal* in 1902, it was later published in Kipling's collected *Just So Stories*. These are part myth, part moral fable, part wry humour, and part children's bedtime fantasy. Most give imaginary explanations of remarkable things – including the essential aloneness of cats.

Kipling's Cat will not give up its independent way of life, even in return for a comfortable Home and Food, as supplied – and controlled – by Woman. Critics have suggested that Kipling's Cat is an allegory, representing deep human instincts, male sexual desire, artistic integrity and the individual's wish for freedom. Just so? Well, maybe.

But was Kipling correct? Are cats always solitary and aloof? Are they doomed to walk alone, for ever?

A pounce of cats

Unlike dogs, cats are not pack animals. They do not need or expect to relate to other members of their own species for most of the time. A single male or female cat will have individual home and hunting-range territories, and will almost always hunt and kill alone. Even mother cats, who are the most devoted carers for the first few weeks of their kittens' lives, will often drive their youngsters away once they are old enough to fend for themselves.

However, cats living in big cities or densely populated suburbs will often come face to face with many other members of their species. In these circumstances, they will develop ways of surviving alongside other cats through complex social networks and hierarchies; sometimes sharing certain space, sometimes taking great care to avoid each other. As we all know, tomcats range far and wide; neutered males and females stay closer to home and meet a smaller number of cat strangers. However, to quote Kipling again, 'the female of the species is more deadly than the male' when it comes to defending kittens against invaders on her home territory.

Experts in feline behaviour say that, when a kitten leaves its nest for a caring owner, it will transfer its infantile needs for food and comfort from its mother to the human. In emotional terms it will remain immature for the rest of its life, at least when relating to humans. Even so, it will never learn to obey random human commands such as 'Sit!' or 'Fetch!' like a dog, or go for a walk with a human owner, or perform useful tasks (except catching mice) – unless it chooses to do so. And as for meetings with other cats, instinctive, mature, feline 'untamed' behaviour will inevitably take over.

Owners can, with patience and a system of rewards, train pet cats to modify their natural behaviour, for example, by using a litter tray. And some cats will observe humans, copy them, and learn to open doors or turn water-taps. But they do this to meet needs that they themselves have identified, or perhaps just for their own amusement.

"

Happy is the home with at least one cat.

Italian proverb

"

CHAPTER FOUR

EVERY HOUSE IS INCOMPLETE WITHOUT HIM

Christopher Smart

The cat sat on the mat. What could possibly be more domestic? That old phrase from children's reading books conjures up an ideal image of household cosiness and peace. The glowing fire, the soft woolly rug, a comfortable chair, a good book, perhaps a cup of tea… Plus, of course, a cat. A pretty, purring friend, sitting nearby and neatly with paws folded and tail wrapped round, or stretched out and basking in the warmth of the flames. A cat, the heart, the soul, of the home. A companion animal.

Even translated into 21st-century terms – cats lounging across warm laptops, leaving paw prints on the screen and fluff trapped among the keys – such an image still seems homely. But, in fact, cats were some of the last animals to be domesticated. They are not natural home-bodies. By nature shy, cautious and defensive, many cat species (apart from lions) lead solitary lives. Often, each wild cat has its own exclusive territory, and will fight to keep other cats out of it, except during the mating season.

As we have seen, cats evolved to need a specialised, protein-rich diet – not normally found among human households. And, unlike dogs, they usually show little interest in learning to perform useful actions when commanded by humans. Since cats only hunt when they choose, they are actually less efficient at controlling mice and rats than are eager dogs like terriers, or animals that naturally kill much more than they need to eat, such as ferrets.

Making friends

In the past, historians used to think that cats were first domesticated in ancient Egypt, a land famous for growing corn that might well need protection from rodent attack. Certainly, ancient Egyptian people admired cats, kept them as pets, and, in certain circumstances, honoured them as living images of a goddess. Egyptian artists and craftworkers also created many wonderful images of felines. Tame house cats appear in Egyptian tomb-paintings from around 3600 BC. But recently, archaeology, combined with genetic studies, has revealed that cats were linked to humans long before ancient Egyptian times – and that they may have chosen to 'domesticate' themselves.

The earliest evidence of cat–human relations comes from the island of Cyprus in the Mediterranean Sea. In 2004, archaeologists investigating a Neolithic (Stone Age) settlement at Shillourokambos discovered the skeleton of a high-status person who had been buried there around 9,500 years ago, together with treasures such as polished stone axes and tools made of flint. Close by was another valuable item: the skeleton of a young cat. It had been carefully laid to rest alongside the dead human. Perhaps it was a pet, perhaps a rare and prized possession. In either case, the cat seems to have been deliberately killed and buried.

Cats are not native to Cyprus, and so the buried animal, or its ancestors, must have been carried there by boat by humans. On close examination, the skeleton turned out to be much larger than modern household pets, and very similar to an African wildcat: *Felis sylvestris lybica*. Three years later, in 2007, scientists at Oxford University, England, published the results of their investigations* into the genetics of wild *Felis sylvestris* subspecies from different parts of the world. They also compared these wildcat genes with those from modern pet cats (*Felis sylvestris catus*). They found overwhelming evidence that today's pet cats are all descended from *Felis sylvestris lybica*, the Near Eastern wildcat. This was the same subspecies as the pet – or prized – cat buried long ago on Cyprus.

* http://www.pnas.org/content/106/suppl.1/9971.full

Five lives

The Oxford scientists had yet more knowledge to share. And it was very surprising. Using mitochondrial DNA (passed down from mother mammals to their offspring), they discovered that all domestic cats in the modern world were descended from just five female Near Eastern wildcats (*Felis sylvestris lybica*). They suggested that each of these five feline 'matriarchs' had started to breed separately, any time between 155,000 and 107,000 years ago.

This evidence from Oxford scientists also makes us think again about how cats came to live in human houses. In short, it seems that they domesticated themselves! The first settled farming communities that we know of were built in the Near East around 11,000 years ago. The farmers stored grain, and mice moved into their barns (archaeologists have found mouse skeletons). Near East wildcats would, at first, have been scared and timid, but, over the centuries, might also have discovered that a human settlement meant a plentiful supply of mice to catch and eat.

Slowly, Near East wildcats learned to tolerate humans, and, later, become friends with them. The Oxford researchers think this happened in several different places and on several different occasions, but that always the descendants of the 'first five females' were involved. Over the generations, cats that had learned to tolerate humans would be sure of a more plentiful food supply. They would thrive, prosper, and multiply. Their descendants – by now, tame or semi-tame, but still bearing DNA from one of the first five females – might later be carried to different places by human settlers or traders, as must have happened for the buried cat to reach the island of Cyprus. In places where there was a local wildcat subspecies, the newcomers would have competed with them for food supplies, and lessened any possibility that the local cats might, in turn, one day become tame.

So: cats moved in, humans tolerated them, found them useful as killers, and maybe even grew to like them. Psychologists have speculated that a cat's babylike features – big eyes, rounded face, high forehead, small nose – might have unconsciously triggered feelings of protectiveness or affection among farmers and their families. To most people, a cats' soft, warm fur is pleasant and comforting to touch; kittens – if you can catch one – love to play.

Gods and pets

The rest, as they say, is history. From paintings, statues, ruined temples, hieroglyph carvings, written law-codes and descriptions by outsiders, we know that the Egyptians honoured cats as representations of divine powers. In art, cats might also symbolise the forces of good order fighting against spiritual chaos. Egyptian households kept pet cats from around 1500 BC, although at first they were for elite families only. Cats were not widespread as pets until after around 660 BC. In theory, the killing of a cat was punishable by death, although we do not know how often this happened. The only recorded person to die for this crime was a Roman soldier, and the Egyptian mob that tore him limb from limb may have had a rather different agenda. Nor do we know how frequently Egyptians mourned the loss of pet cats by shaving off their eyebrows as, – according to Greek writer Herodotus (lived around 450 BC) – the law also required. However, one incident reported by him may just perhaps have been true: when Persian armies invaded Egypt the soldiers used cats as 'feline shields', knowing that the Egyptians would be reluctant to hurl spears at them.

Egyptian cat deities ranged from bloodthirsty Sekhmet – portrayed as a lioness – to fertility goddess Bastet (also the protector of kings and workmen), who was sometimes charmingly pictured as a cat with kittens. Priests at Bast's temple kept tame sacred cats, and worshippers left hundreds of thousands of mummified cats as offerings for the goddess. Sad to say, around 2,000 years later, the soil where these cats were buried was dug up and shipped to northern England, for use as fertiliser.

Cats move on

Egyptian rulers tried to restrict the export of cats, but they soon spread around the shores of the Mediterranean. Ancient Greeks kept cats, and also martens and weasels, as pets. They often lumped all three species together without distinction, and did not consider them sacred. In myths, they saw cats as companions of Artemis, goddess of hunting and the Moon.

The ancient Romans preferred dogs as pets; for them cats were useful, but untameable. It was said that some Roman legions painted their shields with the image of a fierce, fighting wildcat. Even at home, pet cats killed other favourite Roman creatures, especially little birds. In Roman myths, cats accompany the goddess Libertas (Liberty). They are wild and free. Only Roman farmers and sailors valued cats, as rodent-catchers.

"

The fear of you and the dread of you shall be upon every beast of the earth . . . into your hand are they delivered.

Genesis, chapter IX, verses 2–3

"

CHAPTER FIVE

AN UNCLEAN AND IMPURE BEAST

Edward Topsell, 1607

As the old rhyme reminds us, ('*Remember, remember the Fifth of November, Gunpowder, treason and plot...*') on 5 November 1603, a group of Catholic conspirators led by Guy Fawkes plotted to blow up England's King James I as he attended a meeting of Parliament in Westminster. Their plans were discovered and the plot was foiled, but it left a lasting impression. Even today, we still burn 'guys' on bonfires; our fireworks, however, are a later addition.

In the years that followed Guy Fawkes' plot there was little chance of forgetting. There had been distrust and sometimes violence between people in the British Isles holding different religious opinions ever since King Henry VIII had declared himself head of the Church in England in 1533. In the 17th century, these mutual suspicions increased, fanned by the policies and personalities of several English rulers, and by news of bloody religious wars on the continent of Europe. By the 1670s, feelings ran dangerously high.

What has all this to do with cats? Well, the Gunpowder Plot gave rise to a new tradition: Bonfire Night. Today we are used to propping scarecrow-like figures of 'Guys' on the top of our bonfires, but in the 17th century, Protestants often preferred to burn wickerwork effigies of the Pope. Crowds gathered, beer and wine flowed, flames leapt high into the November evening, and a good time was had by all. In periods of particular religious tension, 'pope-makers' (a skilled trade, in London) added a lifelike extra feature to the figures they crafted for burning: they stuffed them with real live cats before setting them on fire.

A Londoner describes the events of November 1677

Last Saturday the [anniversary of the] coronation of Queen Elizabeth was solemnized in the city with mighty bonfires and the burning of a most costly pope, carried by four persons in diverse habits, and the effigies of two devils whispering in his ears, his belly filled with live cats who squalled most hideously as soon as they felt fire; the commons saying all the while it was the language of the pope and the devil in a dialogue betwist them…

Quoted in O. W. Furley, 'The Pope-Burning Processions of the Late Seventeenth Century.' *History*, XLIX No. 44 (1959), p. 17

On this occasion, Gunpowder Plot bonfires were combined with celebrations commemorating the day Elizabeth I had become queen, also early in November, in 1558. To 17th-century Protestants, Elizabeth was something of a religious heroine.

Routine cruelty

Seventeenth-century Londoners were not alone in being horrible to cats. Evidence of cats being tortured to provide sound-effects for tableaux and pageants can be found in many parts of Europe from at least 200 years earlier. Cats were locked in cages with their tails trapped to create 'cat organs' or 'cat pianos'. When the 'player' pressed the organ keys they crushed each cat's tail in turn, making it yowl. At the New Year, cats (perhaps representing evil spirits, or the old year) might be hunted with hounds and killed for fun; at Midsummer, they were burnt on bonfires. At spring and autumn fairs, they were hung up in baskets or leather bottles and shot at, as a game, for target practice.

Throughout the UK, cats were trapped and killed for their fur – which was used to trim clothes or make gloves. Few families fed the lean, scrawny moggies that lived around their houses or farms (feeding was said to make them too lazy to catch mice). And, although cats' flesh was normally considered unclean because they ate vermin, cats were caught and eaten at times when food ran short. Usually, cat meat was made into a thick soup, or else sold as 'rabbit'.

When a new house was built, a cat or two might be bricked up in the wall or under the threshold to keep mice away – or maybe evil spirits. In Celtic countries, cats were roasted alive in a ghastly ritual designed to foretell the future. Even nursery rhymes describe cats' casual ill-treatment, by children treating them as toys:

Ding dong bell,
Pussy's in the well.
Who threw her in?
Little Tommy Green.
Who pulled her out?

The Kattenstoet: Cats' Festival

On the second Sunday of May, every three years, the townsfolk of Ypres in Belgium dress up in medieval-style clothes, march through the streets accompanied by bands, flags and giant puppets on stilts, and gather at the foot of the high bell-tower of the city's ancient Cloth Hall. There they wait with outstretched arms while a Kattenstoet official, dressed as a jester, throws – yes, you've guessed – cats down from the top of the tower.

Don't worry! These are toy cats, made of plush or plastic, but the custom of cat-throwing does commemorate ancient traditions of torturing cats as part of 'folkloristic games'. Probably, in the past, cats that had moved into warm, dry shelters like Ypres Cloth Hall for the winter were cleared out each spring, as the buildings were made ready to receive fresh stock in the summer. The cats had done a useful job all winter by keeping mice away. By May, they were surplus to requirements (and had probably produced countless kittens); they had to be disposed of.

Even so, no-one knows exactly why cats were killed for fun. Perhaps, in crowded medieval towns, cats were so plentiful, so little regarded, and so often seen as a nuisance, that they could be used in cruel ways.

Cats, rats, fleas...

In the years between around 1347 and 1660, when attacks of plague killed millions of people in Europe, townspeople believed that cats and dogs spread the disease, and so animals found wandering in the city streets were rounded up and slaughtered.

With hindsight, we can see that this was foolish and counter-productive. Cats killed the rats that carried the fleas that spread Plague bacteria to humans. They did not carry the plague fleas themselves (nor did dogs); the fleas bred on rats only. However, medieval people did not know this, and bacteria had not yet been discovered. And so, by killing cats, they removed one of the few effective weapons they had to combat the deadly infection.

Only a cat?

Looking back at these past practices, we ask: 'How could anyone be so cruel, so beastly?' Basically, because, for hundreds of years, perfectly decent, law-abiding, God-fearing men and women thought that cruelty to cats – or to many other animals – did not matter. Why? In a word, because of their religion. Because of Christianity.

In pre-Christian times, among the Celts of western Europe, myths and legends described cats that could speak. Cats were messengers from the Celtic Otherworld, and sacred to the Moon. Some magic cats or fairy cats, including the great Royal Cat who lived in a cave in Ireland, could even foretell the future. Others guarded secret treasure. A few – like the beautiful Irish princess cursed by her evil stepmother and transformed into an otter, a deer and a cat – were humans who had shape-shifted. Irish folktales also told how evil spirits – perhaps the Devil himself, or perhaps faint memories of Celtic nature-deities – assumed the shape of a giant cat and forced all the other felines in the neighbourhood to obey him. Often, the spirit-cat stirred up wars between different cat clans or villages, for his own amusement.

Later, some of these old tales turned into political parables that (alas!) still featured cat cruelty. One of the most famous described how, when Oliver Cromwell's soldiers occupied the city of Kilkenny in Ireland in 1650, they tied the tails of the local cats together, hung them over a wire, and watched them fight until they died. Since then – or so the story goes – the phrase 'to fight like Kilkenny cats' has come to be applied to people who go on fighting to the bitter end, even if it destroys them.

The lovely goddess

In Norse lands, Viking myths told how Freyja, goddess of fertility and promiscuous love, rode the skies in a golden chariot pulled by two beautiful blue-grey cats. They were so big and heavy that even mighty Thor, god of Thunder, could not lift them – although he himself had given them, a precious treasure, to Freyja, perhaps in return for her favours. Norse writers and visitors to Scandinavia described the native Norwegian forest cat (a local subspecies of *Felis sylvestris catus*), which was famous for its size, strength, beautiful long thick coat and ability to swim. Perhaps Freyja's cats looked like these?

Viking farmers left out gifts for Freyja's cats, hoping she would send a good harvest. Traditionally, Viking brides were presented with gifts of kittens at their weddings – sometimes tucked up neatly in a baby's cradle. The kittens were expected to earn their keep by catching mice, but were also a powerful piece of sympathetic magic. They encouraged the bride's fertility: cats were famous for their uninhibited love-making (see page 152).

Creatures vile?

Traditions like these, from Celtic and Norse lands, persisted in many parts of Europe long after the first missionary priests arrived to spread the Christian message (between AD 500–1100). And so, in early Christian centuries, cats became symbols of the old pagan religions. The Church was keen to quash such 'wicked superstitions' and therefore regarded cats with great suspicion.

Priests and people also quoted passages from the Bible (such as the example on page 82). They understood these texts to mean that God had given humans lordship over brute beasts, and that animals had been created, with divine generosity, for human food, use or pleasure. In England, this attitude was backed up by the law, which declared that cats were of 'a base [low] nature' and 'unclean and impure'. They did not matter, because they were inferior to humans. Even Shakespeare's characters joined in: calling cats 'killing creatures vile' (*Cymbeline*, act 5, scene 5).

The properties of cats

Thirteenth-century friar Bartholomew the Englishman describes cats in his encyclopaedia, *On the Properties of Things*:

He is a full lecherous beast in youth, swift, pliant, and merry, and leapeth and reseth on everything that is to fore him: and is led by a straw, and playeth therewith: and is a right heavy beast in age and full sleepy, and lieth slyly in wait for mice: and is aware where they be more by smell than by sight, and hunteth and reseth on them in privy places: and when he taketh a mouse, he playeth therewith, and eateth him after the play.

In time of love [there] is hard fighting for wives, and one scratcheth and rendeth the other grievously with biting and with claws. And he maketh a ruthful noise and ghastful, when one proffereth to fight with another: and unneth is hurt when he is thrown down off an high place.

And when he hath a fair skin, he is as it were proud thereof, and goeth fast about: and when his skin is burnt, then he bideth at home, and

is oft for his fair skin taken of [by] the skinner,
and slain and flayed.

pliant = bendy
reseth = seizes
to fore = before
is led by = will follow
privy = hidden
rendeth = rips
reseth = grabs, siezes
ruthful = sorrowful
proffereth = threatens
unneth = never
goeth fast about = likes to be out and about
bideth = stays
flayed = skinned

Cited in E. Stock, *Medieval lore* (London:
Robert Steele, 1893)

Living tools

Bartholomew was a keen observer, and there is no evidence that he actively disliked cats, or indeed that he had any feelings about them at all. In everyday life, from Bartholomew's day until almost 1700, cats were most often treated as 'living tools', useful and maybe even essential, but without any rights or feelings. Seventeenth-century diarist Samuel Pepys records the fact that his wife had been given a kitten to rid their house of mice, but he does not say anything more about the animal, or even whether it had a name. In contrast, Pepys writes affectionately about his dog, Fancy, 'one of his oldest acquaintances and servants', and admires his wife's new dog, a spaniel bitch, Flora, who was 'mighty pretty'...

There were some cat-lovers in the centuries between the Vikings and Guy Fawkes. They were devoted to their pet cats and treated them with kindness and sympathy. You can read more about them in Chapter 7. But for one group of people, popular superstitions involving cats combined with the Church's official hostility to the species could be very,

very dangerous. You know who I mean: those poor old wise women/alternative healers/dangerous dabblers in devilry who believed they rode on broomsticks and were famously fond of black cats. Oh, and also anyone else the Church labelled a 'heretic'. If we dare, let's see what happened to them and their feline companions, in the next chapter.

A cat by any other name would scratch as sharp

Cats are cats – in English, and in many other European languages, as well. The French say *chat*, the Spaniards *gatto*, the Greeks *gata* or *gati*, the Russians *kot* and, affectionately, *koshka*. And there is also English *puss*, Dutch *poes*, and Romanian *pisica*. Elswhere, many cat names are based on the noise a cat makes. For example, in ancient Egypt, cats were *miw*, in modern Vietnamese and Cantonese they are *meo* or *maow*. Other cat names are, well, the names for cats as different linguistic families see them. They range from *neko* in Japan and *koyanji* in Korea to Tamil *poonai*, Indonesia *kuching*, and Gujerati *billadi*.

"

Thrice the brindled cat hath
mewed,
Thrice and once the hedge-pig
whined...

Macbeth, act 4, scene 1

brindled = speckled
hedge-pig = hedgehog

William Shakespeare sets the scene for a witches'
Sabbath, using only the best ingredients: 'eye of newt
and toe of frog, wool of bat and tongue of dog...'

"

CHAPTER SIX

BEWARE THE CAT

English writer William Baldwin, book title, 1561

Would you want to kiss a black cat – on its bottom? According to Pope Gregory IX, in 1232, that was the high point (yes, really) of a ceremony conducted by a group of German heretics – people who disobeyed or contradicted the teachings of the Church. According to Gregory, these heretics (male and female) gathered together and joined in a ceremony that involved fondling toads, greeting a strange apparition that looked like a skin-covered skeleton, sharing a meal, kissing the aforementioned cat as it advanced, tail first, and afterwards murmuring *We know, master* and *We must obey.*

Over 250 years later, in 1484, at the start of
what became known as the European witch
craze, a later Pope, Innocent VII, wrote that:

> ...it has recently come to our ears, not without
> great pain to us, that in some parts of upper
> Germany...many persons of both sexes, heedless
> of their own salvation and forsaking the Catholic
> faith, give themselves over to devils male and
> female, and by their incantations, charms,
> and conjurings, and by other abominable
> superstitions and sortileges, offences, crimes, and
> misdeeds, ruin and cause to perish the offspring
> of women, the foal of animals, the products of the
> earth, the grapes of vines, and the fruits
> of trees...

sortileges = fortune-tellings; dealings with ghosts

Even if such ceremonies and conjurings did
take place – and it is far more likely that they
happened only in the fevered imaginations of
witch-finders and heretic-hunters – why
should they involve cats? What was going on?

Magic all around

First and foremost, people believed in witches. Even intelligent, well-educated people with access to top scholars and the best libraries, like Scotland's King James VI = England's King James I. He suspected that witches had raised storms to kill him on his wedding voyage between Scotland and Denmark; and he wrote a popular book on witchcraft. People also believed that there were supernatural forces at work in the world. If good, these came from God; if bad, they came from the Devil.

Good or bad, this magic was powerful. Witch-hunters and many other perfectly normal people felt convinced that devil-worshippers could transform themselves into strange creatures, especially cats, through rituals, spells or potions – like the ghastly brew concocted by Shakespeare's three witches. To protect themselves from these dangerous visitors, householders were advised to sprinkle salt across the threshold of their front door. But they still believed folktales such as these:

• The house and workshop belonging to a carpenter in the Highlands were infested with cats. The carpenter's servant girl swore she could hear them talking to each other. That night, the carpenter attacked the cats with his knife, dirk (dagger) and broadsword. They scattered, but next morning, two local women, reputed to be witches, died of mysterious injuries.

• A Yorkshire farmer was riding home late one night. He came to a bridge, where he was bewitched by a local old woman. For over an hour, neither he nor his horse could move one inch, until a villager happened along, with a strong rowan walking stick in his hand. (Rowan trees were famous for their power against bad magic.) The witch ran away – in the shape of a black cat – and a farmer and his horse were able to continue their journey.

At the same time, the everyday natural world was also full of signs and messages from Heaven or Hell; these could take the form of monstrous births or sudden storms, or might be carried by animals. Cats were the usual suspects: unlike dogs and horses, they did not readily obey human commands. As some witch-hunters saw it, by ignoring human authority cats were challenging the divine order of the world.

Witch-hunting!

When times were bad, it was tempting to think that someone you disliked, despised or feared had been trying to manipulate these forces, to help themselves or harm others. You called that person a witch and subjected them to torture, or at best to humiliating investigations. And you accused them of receiving visits from evil spirits or devils or 'familiars':

> …another witch…was thereupon apprehended, and searched by women, who had for many years known the devil's marks, and found to have three teats about her, which honest women have not: so upon command from the Justice, they were to keep her from sleep two or three nights, expecting in that time to see her familiars…

Matthew Hopkins, *Discovery of Witches*, 1647

Since cats were common visitors to many peoples' houses, and since many witches were poor, old, ill or powerless people who lived alone on the margins of society and looked to animals for companionship, cats were the creatures most commonly associated with witchcraft. But they were not the only ones. After four days and nights of sleep deprivation, the supposed witch investigated by Matthew Hopkins admitted to having – or maybe hallucinated – familiars that took the shapes of a white kitten, a spaniel, a greyhound, a rabbit and a polecat. The idea that witches' cats have to be black is a modern invention, perhaps coming from the USA, along with many Halloween customs.

Pusse, I will curse thee…

Scholar and poet Thomas Master, 1603–1643.
(He changed his mind …)

• In 1566, it was reported that Elizabeth Francis, an alleged witch from Chelmsford in southeast England, had a cat named Sathan. He was white, and it was claimed that she fed him with drops of her blood. Sathan was accused of stealing cattle, working love-magic, committing multiple murders, and transforming himself into a poisonous toad.

• In 1619, Lincolnshire woman Margaret Flower was accused of witchcraft. It was said that she took items belonging to children whom she wished to harm, and rubbed the stolen goods against her cat's body. It was also said that she did the same with a feather taken from a noblewoman's bed, to make that lady infertile.

• In Hungary, people long ago were reported to cut crosses in a cat's skin, to stop it turning into a witch.

• If a child was sick because of suspected witchcraft, its nurse grabbed a cat by all four legs, swung it round and threw it out of the house. She was throwing the witch's magic out with it. If the cat died, the child would (supposedly) live.

• One test to see whether a cat was a witch was to throw it into a bowl of holy water. If the cat tried to escape, it was guilty.

Witches into cats

Of course (so past people believed) witches could also turn themselves into cats:

Also, the changing of witches into hares, cats and the like shapes, is so common as late testimonies and confessions approve [prove] unto us, that none but the stupidly incredulous can wrong the credit of the the reporters, or doubt of the certainty...

Edward Fairfax, *Daemonologica: A Discourse of Witchcraft*, 1621

Thou shalt not suffer a witch to live.

Exodus, chapter 22 verse 18

Towards the end of the medieval era, as we have seen, the Church – the most influential, best-educated and widest-reaching organisation in Europe – joined in, or even led, movements of mass hysteria about witchcraft. Kings, queens and city councillors also expressed concern about the supposed damage sorcery could do to civil society in this world and to individual souls in the next. For over 300 years, there were witch trials and outbreaks of public panic throughout Europe, and, later, in European colonies in North America. As many as 40,000 alleged witches, mostly women, were killed, together with an unknown number of cats. The cats were burned to death or hanged, just like their owners.

At last, after 1700, the craze for witch-hunting died down. But many, many superstitions concerning cats and their supposed occult powers lived on. Some are still current today:

• Do not discuss family secrets or important business in front of a cat. It might be a witch in disguise, and will overhear you.

• You can make the wind blow by shutting a cat up in a cupboard.

• If a cat sits with its back to the fire, there will be a frost.

• If a cat washes with its foot behind its ear, or takes extra trouble to clean its face and whiskers, then it's going to rain.

• Kittens born in May – a magic month – will bring 'devilish' creatures such as snakes into the house.

• Black cats contain a 'lucky' bone. If the cat is killed – by boiling water! – the bone will protect the killer.

• Black cats are lucky (UK); black cats are unlucky (USA).

- Anyone who kills a cat sells their soul to the Devil.

- It is unlucky if a black cat crosses your path, unless you spit at it.

- It is unlucky to meet a cat on the morning of your wedding.

- It is lucky if a black cat pays a visit to your house.

- It's bad luck to purchase a cat, good luck to receive one as a gift.

- A cat will suck the breath out of a sleeping person's body.

- A cat's breath is poisonous.

- It's unhealthy to let the cat sleep on the bed.

- If a kitten and a baby are born on the same day, the baby is doomed to die young.

- It is bad luck if a cat walks over the lap of a pregnant woman.

- Don't let a cat walk across a corpse or a coffin. The next person who sees it will go blind.

Curious cat cures

Readers, we implore you NOT to try any of these at home. They would be dangerous for patients, and harming a cat is strictly illegal.

• To remove a spell cast by a witch on a child, take the heart of a black cat and hit the child seven times with it on the face and the navel. Then roast the heart, and feed the child with bits of this at suppertime for seven consecutive days. N.B. The cat must be the seventh in a litter, and seven years old. The remains of the heart, if thrown into a witch's home, will give her terrible stomach pains.

• Roast the head of a pure-black cat until it crumbles into powder. Blow this into your eyes to cure infections.

• The powered gall-bladder of a black cat can cure convulsions.

• Got a badly infected finger? Stick it into a cat's ear for a cure.

• Cat skin worn across the stomach takes away aches and pains.

• Blood from a cut-off cat's tail can cure shingles.

• Rubbing with a live cat's tail will cure styes (infections of the eyelids).

• Hairs from a black cat, chopped, soaked in water and swallowed, will cure whooping cough.

• In Ireland, the blood of a black cat was thought to be a fail-safe cure for scabies – an itchy, disfiguring and highly contagious skin disease caused by tiny mites (creatures related to spiders).

• Among pioneer settlers in the USA, a cat skin was reckoned to be a cure for rheumatism.

Cats and the sea

Cats have travelled on board ship since ancient Egyptian times. They were taken on wild-fowling expeditions by Egyptian nobles, and were carried on cargo ships laden with grain to catch stowaway mice. Merchant ships sailed by Phoenicians from the East Mediterranean probably carried cats to many coastal areas of northern Europe – maybe even the British Isles – after around 900 BC. Roman, Celtic, Viking and medieval sailors all had cats on board. The first domestic cats were taken to the Americas by European explorers and settlers in the late 16th and 17th centuries.

As well as catching rats and mice that ate food stores and chewed ropes and sails, cats were believed to have supernatural powers to control the weather:

• Cats could call up winds, especially at sea.

• A playful cat on board ship was a bad omen: 'the wind was in her tail'. It meant a bad storm was approaching.

• It was bad luck for fishermen to speak the word 'cat' while preparing their lines with bait. The first man to hear the word might die.

• If a cat played with a sailor's wife's apron, a gale would blow.

And many, many more.

Pirate cats – and spies

Black cats are viewed with suspicion in many parts of the world. But it's only in southern Italy that a seafaring story is offered as the reason why. Traditional tales tell how black cats first landed from the ships of ruthless Barbary Pirates (based in Algeria and active between around 1500 and 1800) and how the cats were either left behind by accident when the pirates sailed away, or else were 'planted' on land to serve as the pirates' spies. True or false as such stories may be, black cats are still not popular in Italy. Since 2007, the Italian Association for the Defence of Animals and the Environment has celebrated a 'Black Cat Day' every year (on 27 November), to ask all Italians not to harm them.

66

The harmless, necessary cat...

William Shakespeare, *Merchant of Venice*, act 4, scene 1

99

CHAPTER SEVEN

FURRY FRIENDS?

Some time around AD 800, an Irish monk, working late in his cell in a draughty monastery on an island in Lake Constance, Austria, mused on the parallels between his own existence and the life of his companion, a cat named Pangur Ban. (Say 'Pang-gaar Bawn'; it means 'White Washer.)'

Hunting mice is his delight,
Hunting words I sit all night.

transl. Robin Flower in
Poems and Translations, Constable, 1931.
By permission of The Lilliput Press, Dublin

To write his poem, the monk used Gaelic, the language of his family and childhood, rather than the scholarly Latin of the Church. This suggests that he was writing intimately, from the heart. His poem admires Pangur Bán's single-minded concentration and treats the cat with respect, as a creature with its own wishes and intentions. Pangur Bán is not a pet; but neither is he vermin, or mindless or worthless – or demonic.

Six hundred years later, shortly before 1400, England's most famous medieval poet, Geoffrey Chaucer, described one very well-treated moggie. But cosy and comfortable as that cat's life was, it could not suppress its basic instinct, to go hunting:

> Or take a cat, and feed him well with milk
> And tender flesh, and make his bed of silk,
> And [= But] let him see a mouse go by the wall;
> At once he leaves the milk and flesh and all
> And every dainty that is in that house,
> Such appetite has he to eat a mouse.
> Desire has here its mighty power shown,
> And inborn appetite reclaims its own.

Geoffrey Chaucer, *Canterbury Tales*, 'The Manciple's Tale', lines 175–182

Cats have friends

Chaucer was not really writing about cats; he was telling a human story with a moral message. But he assumes that his audience will recognise the image of a pampered pet. In the same way, late-medieval books of instruction on good manners from several European countries sternly warn guests in castles and other grand dining halls not to play with pet cats at the dinner-table. It seems clear that, in spite of what we have read about the fear, loathing and ill-treatment excited by many cats during the Middle Ages, there were some cat-lovers around.

Although the records are patchy and distorted, the names of several famous people who enjoyed the companionship of cats have survived. Here are just a few:

• **St Gertrude of Nivelles** (AD 626–659) – head of a community of nuns in the Low Countries (now Belgium). Like many nuns, she had a pet cat (although dogs – too devoted, too demonstrative – were not allowed). Miraculously, the bread baked in Gertrude's oven and the water from her well were reported to repel mice and rats.

• **St Francis of Assisi** (1182–1226) – Italian helper of the poor, mystic who saw God in all creation, patron saint of animals. Legends tell how he was saved from a plague of mice by a cat that miraculously appeared from his sleeve.

• **Francesco Petrarca** (1304–1374) – Italian poet, traveller and scholar. Famous for helping to revive interest in ancient Roman civilisation, and for a tragic, unrequited love-affair. Some stories say that Petrarch was even more devoted to his cat than to his dead sweetheart, Laura. Its mummified body is still on display in the ancient house near Padua where he lived and worked towards the end of his life.

• **Julian of Norwich** (1342–1416) – Christian mystic and anchorite (hermit), who lived in eastern England. She kept a cat in her cell, perhaps for company, perhaps to scare mice away.

• **Joachim du Bellay** (1522–1560), pioneer of classicising poetry in the French language. He owned – and loved – one of the first blue-grey 'Chartreux' cats ever recorded. When it died in 1558, he was heartbroken:

…Now my life is a misery…
It's not because I've lost my rings, my coins, my
   purse.
What are they worth?
No – it's because three days ago I lost
My pet, my love, my delight.
Who? What? Oh, cruel memory!
My heart trembles whenever I
   talk of it, or write.
My Belaud, my little grey cat.
Belaud, who was, I bet,
The finest cat that nature
Ever created …

(author's translation)

• **Henry Wriothesley**, 3rd earl of Southampton (1573–1642) – courtier, soldier, entrepreneur, overseas trader, patron of William Shakespeare and possibly his lover, 'A man right fair' [= handsome]. After taking part in a political conspiracy that failed, Lord Southampton was imprisoned in the Tower of

London under sentence of death – along with his black and white cat. It is shown in a famous portrait of him, sitting on the prison window sill. They were both later released.

• **Archbishop William Laud** (1573–1645) – scholar, linguist, lawyer; leader of the Church of England during a time of violent religious quarrels. Supported King Charles I during the Civil War, and was beheaded. Famously workaholic, sharp-tongued and bad-tempered; his only close friends seem to have been cats. It was reported that he owned one of the first Cyprus (tabby) cats imported to England. The name 'tabby' is Arabic: it comes from striped silk originally produced in the district of Attabiy, Baghdad, Iraq. Archbishop Laud collected Arabic manuscripts, and, it seems, cats as well.

• **Armand du Plessis, Cardinal Richelieu** (1585–1642) – prince of the Church, politician, soldier, diplomat, patron of the arts and, for a while, the most powerful man in France. Advisor to King Louis XIII. At his death, he owned 14 cats, of many different breeds. One historian has suggested that high-ranking people at the royal courts of Europe lived in luxury but were emotionally deprived. They looked to pets, preferably exotic, rare and beautiful, such as Cardinal Richelieu's long-haired Angora cat, to fill the gap in their lives.

Harmless? Necessary?

There may, of course, have been a great many other, less exalted, men and women who liked cats, but we do not know their names. Early writers, who all came from privileged, well-educated ranks in society, assumed that top people kept pets, while peasants – themselves rather swinish – simply lived alongside animals. That is not strictly true. The cats that chased mice and sat beside the fire in farm cottages and city streets may not have been indulged and petted. But many of them were valued – so long as they earned their keep.

The rats by night such mischief did,
Betty [the maid] was every morning chid:
They undermined whole sides of bacon,
Her cheese was sapp'd, her tarts were taken;
Her pasties, fenced with thickest paste,

Were all demolished, and laid waste:
She cursed the Cat, for want of duty…

John Gay, *The Rat Catcher and Cats*, 1769

However, as Shakespeare wrote, at least some people considered working cats both 'harmless' and 'necessary'. In Wales, for example, around AD 942, famous lawmaker King Hywel Dda (the Good) passed laws compelling anyone who killed a cat to pay a heavy fine. The cat was held up by the tip of its tail, and the offender had to hand over enough grain to make a mound that completely covered it. Compared with a trained hunting dog, Hywel's laws did not prize cats highly – they were about one-thirtieth of a good dog's value – but they were still worth about the same as a sheep or a goat. English laws also valued cats for their usefulness. King Edward III (reigned 1327–1377) decreed that every English merchant ship must have a cat on board, presumably to protect its export cargoes of wool or grain from rodents. Further English laws, regulating profits taken from salvaged shipwrecks, stipulated that a vessel could not be considered truly abandoned if a cat or a dog was still alive among the wreckage. Even so, ideas that cats spread plague continued, for a while. In 1512, the city council in Edinburgh, Scotland, ordered the immediate execution of all stray cats, dogs and pigs as soon as fresh cases of the infection appeared. The fate of pet cats is not mentioned, but the law makes a distinction between stray and cared-for animals. This suggests that attitudes to pets were changing.

Pets and people

Travellers in English towns and guests at country houses throughout the 16th and 17th centuries, remarked on the number of cats that they saw, indoors and out. Sometimes, these pets caused 'nastiness' inside a room, to the disgust of fastidious visitors. But around 1630, John Harrison, a merchant from Leeds in northern England, was reported to have solved this problem. He paid to have holes made in some of the doors of his house, so that his cats could come and go freely. Perhaps the first recorded cat-flaps!

At the same time, people were beginning to suggest that cats might perhaps care about their human owners. What if they had some kind of consciousness, or even feelings? In 1605, clergyman Edward Topsell (died 1635) published an English translation of *Historia Animalium* (*the History of Animals*) by Swiss naturalist, Conrad Gesner. It contained this passage:

> ...(the cat's) loving nature to man, how she flattereth by rubbing her skin against one's legs, how she whurleth with her voice...she hath one voice to beg and to complain, another to testifie her delight and pleasure.... Therefore how she beggeth, playeth, leapeth, looketh, catcheth, tosseth with her foot, riseth up to strings held over her head, sometimes creeping, sometimes lying on the back, playing with one foot, sometime on the belly ...

testifie = show

Gesner and Topsell might have been wrong in interpreting all these actions as signs of genuine love ('whatever that means'), but they certainly thought that their cats were capable of being pleased to see them. And in France, brilliant philosopher Michel de Montaigne (1533–1592) was also asking startling new questions about a cat's mental processes:

> When I am enjoying a game with my cat, who knows whether she has more fun playing with me than I have playing with her?

As we saw in Chapter 6, routine and deliberate ill-treatment of cats continued for a good 100 years after Montaingne's thoughtful query. But, slowly, very slowly, a new age was beginning.

God's Creation

Meanwhile, in the Middle East, the original homeland of domestic cats, the faith of Islam taught that all creation should be respected. Indeed, the natural world was full of signs of God. The Muslim holy scripture, the Qur'an, teaches that every animal has its God-given place in creation. God sees and knows them all – and all will be 'gathered to their Lord'* at the end of time.

*The Qur'an, 6:38

One Muslim tradition records the Prophet Muhammad (AD 570–632) saying: 'Whoever is kind to the creatures of God is kind to God himself.' And a popular story, setting an example of good behaviour for Muslims to follow, tells how when the Prophet came to put on his robe one day, he found a favourite cat, Muezza, sleeping on it. Rather than disturb her, the Prophet cut the sleeve off his robe, and went to say his prayers. When he returned, Muezza was awake, and thanked him.

Have tail, will travel

From the time of the ancient Greeks and Romans – or even earlier – descendants of the first five female cats (see page 77) were carried east. Some became settled in Anatolia (now Turkey), the Caucasus Mountains and Iran; domestic cats have been found in archaeological deposits there dating from around 2000 BC. Some time after that, a genetic mutation appeared, creating the long-haired 'Persian' cats – which first appeared in Europe (as exotic rarities) from around 1600.

Cats seem to have reached the Indus Valley and the Indian subcontinent, carried by traders along the ancient Silk Road. According to some Indian traditions, early Hindu rulers required every house to have a cat – presumably for pest control. Cats also lived with priests at Hindu and Buddhist temples.

From India, Buddhist missionaries took cats to China and South-East Asia between around 200 BC and AD 400. As rare and valuable imports, cats became the pets of rich and powerful people or else (as in India and Europe) lived with religious communities and scholars. In Siam (Thailand), Burma (Myanmar) and nearby lands, sacred cats were kept in temples, where they protected precious religious manuscripts from rats and mice. Devout Buddhists also believed that when a person of spiritual merit died, their soul passed into one of the temple cats. It remained there until the cat was dead, after which the soul was freed from all earthly cares or desires, and achieved Nirvana.

'Colour-pointed' and 'silver' cats, looking rather like today's Siamese and Korat breeds, became the prized possessions of the kings of Siam. These elegant creatures lived carefully guarded lives at the royal court, and their beauties were celebrated in a famous manuscript: *Tamra Maew* (*Cat-Book Poems*). Compiled some time between 1350 and 1767, it is perhaps the oldest book in praise of cats. The original text is in delicate verse:

> ...her fur is the colour
> of a cloud,
> Her eyes shine like dewdrops
> on a lotus leaf....

Source: http://www.thai-blogs.com/2005/10/08/the-royal-cats-of-siam/

It describes seventeen lucky cats and some less auspicious ones, and is illustrated with lifelike paintings. Later, Korat cats were offered as generous wedding gifts to wealthy, high-ranking couples in South-East Asia. Their silver-grey fur symbolised riches.

Rare and precious

Further north, in China and Japan, cat ownership was at first restricted by law to emperors and prestigious monasteries. Cats were kept on leads and never allowed to step beyond safe protective walls. This meant that they were disliked by ordinary men and women – until their rulers relented, and farmers and silk-weavers welcomed cats into their homes as useful hunters of mice.

But the link between cats and royalty also meant that cat stories became a safe way of spreading gossip about powerful people. Chinese Empress Wu Zetian (AD 625–705), a truly remarkable ruler, was also a wicked stepmother, conspirator, murderer and much more. Stories were told how one of Wu's victims cursed her before she died, saying that she would return to haunt Wu in the shape of a cat, turn Wu into a rat, and devour her. Wu was not deterred and went ahead with the execution, but (so the story said) she had all the palace cats killed as well, just to be on the safe side.

66

The question is not, Can they [animals] reason? nor, Can they talk? but, Can they suffer?

Jeremy Bentham, *Introduction to the Principles of Morals and Legislation*, 1789, revised 1823

99

CHAPTER EIGHT

THE SMALLEST FELINE IS A MASTERPIECE

Leonardo da Vinci (1452–1519)

There's nowt so queer as folk, or so they say, and few 'folk' were more peculiar than lawyer, philosopher and pioneer sociologist, Jeremy Bentham (1748–1832). Very, very clever and distinctly eccentric (he asked for his dead body to be preserved and put on display in a glass case at University College London, where it can still be seen), Bentham asked new and unusual questions, about animals as well as people. At the time, Bentham's concern for animal suffering (page 130) was considered by many to be just another of his oddities. Today, we would probably admire him: 'Well said, Jeremy!'

However strange, Bentham was far from mad. He campaigned for social reform using strictly rational reasoning. He aimed to bring about the best living conditions for the largest number of people. To his mind, that meant giving the law's protection to 'any sensitive [= conscious, feeling] being', including animals. Bentham was not being sentimental about pussy-cats and other pets; just legal and logical. He argued that an adult horse or dog had better-developed consciousness than a newborn human. Therefore, unless the law protected horses, dogs and other living, feeling creatures, it could not be used to protect babies.

A change of view

As late as 1637, Europe's leading intellectual, French mathematician and philosopher René Descartes, had argued that because animals lacked moral or intellectual consciousness, they could not feel pain. So it did not matter how humans treated them. But by Bentham's day, the systematic observation and classification of the natural world was leading many scientists to think differently. In

1794, Erasmus Darwin (famous doctor, naturalist and inventor grandfather of the still more famous Charles Darwin) asked:

> Does not daily observation convince us that they [animals] form contracts of friendship with each other, and with mankind?

Certainly, Jeremy Bentham had 'contracts of friendship' with his cats. He annoyed many of his human acquaintances by allowing cats to sit, on chairs, around his dining table – especially his favourite, a tom that he named 'The Reverend Sir John Langbourne, Doctor of Divinity'. Few other cat-lovers went so far as that, but, from around 1700, cats, dogs and all kinds of other pets took up residence in better-off homes. They also featured in newly fashionable 'affective' literature, based on personal opinions, emotions and sensations.

From the early 1700s, cats crop up in countless letters, diaries, poems, stories, and descriptions of family life. For example, when Selima, the cat belonging to art-loving MP Horace Walpole, drowned in a bowl of pet goldfish, Walpole's friend, poet Thomas Gray (1717–1761), wrote an elegant lament to console him. It is still remembered today, for its famous last line: 'All that glisters is not gold.' Dr Samuel Johnson (1709–1784), compiler of the first great English dictionary, also had a favourite cat, named Hodge. That, too, was remembered in (truly terrible) verse:

> Who, by his master when caressed,
> Warmly his gratitude expressed,
> And never failed his thanks to purr,
> Whene'er he stroked his sable fur.

Percival Stockdale (1736–1811)

– but also by Johnson's biographer, Scottish diarist James Boswell, in 1778. Boswell was not a cat lover, and reminds us that only people with money and leisure could truly devote themselves to their pets: 'I never shall forget the indulgence with which he [Johnson] treated Hodge, his cat: for whom he himself used to go out and buy oysters, lest the servants having that trouble should take a dislike to the poor creature…' Servants working for masters like Johnson and Boswell often came from very poor homes, where food for humans was in short supply. It is perhaps not surprising that they had no time for pet fads and fancies.

Cat facts, cat fictions

Across the Channel, French writer François-Augustin de Paradis de Moncrif won unexpected fame with a 'grave and fanciful' book, *Les Chats* (*The Cats*, 1727). It began almost as a literary game; its 20th-century translator called it 'an imaginative literary probe into the nature of the feline'. But it turned into the first book in Europe solely devoted to cats, even if its contents cannot always be guaranteed to be true. Cat-lovers took it seriously, although some of Moncrif's fellow-authors started to greet him with a mocking 'Miaou' rather than 'Bonjour'.

Moncrif delighted in telling strange anecdotes, such as the tale of Mademoiselle Dupuy, who played the harp. She believed that she owed her musical talents to her cat and insisted that it sit beside her and criticise her performances. Mlle Dupuy was so grateful for this 'help' that when she died, shortly before 1700, she left her houses and fortune to her pet. Her relatives later contested the will – and won.

Not long after Moncrif, another Frenchman, the Comte de Buffon, began to publish his masterwork: *Natural History*. It ran to 36 volumes (1749–1788) and became required reading 'for every educated man in Europe'. Buffon's text contained scientific descriptions of the natural world, together with beautifully detailed pictures. Buffon did not like cats, but he was a brilliant observer, and his book contains some of the earliest accurate images of separate breeds of cats, clearly displaying their anatomical differences.

A new image

Buffon's *Natural History* viewed cats from a scientific point of view. But, by the time it was published, many other people in Europe, Russia, South-East Asia, China and especially Japan, were creating pictures of cats because they liked the look of the species. In the Middle Ages (as in Roman times), artists had often used cats as symbols of natural-born wickedness: cats catching birds, chasing mice. In paintings from Christian countries, they are even shown turning away from the Virgin

Mary or baby Jesus, just like unrepentant human sinners. From around 1450, artists made detailed studies of cats and many other curiously shaped animals that were difficult to draw. Some, like Leonardo (see page 130), also marvelled at cats' beauty.

Over the next 200 years, images of cats changed from demonic to decorative. Sometimes, we can see this transition at work – for example, in a famous, rather sobering, painting, *The Graham Children*, completed by British artist William Hogarth in 1742. This group portrait features four beautiful children and a pretty tabby cat, surrounded by images of love and death. The cat has its eyes firmly fixed on a toy bird in a cage, eager to snatch it and devour it – just as death snatched away one of the children shown in the painting before the work was even finished.

This shifting image of cats moved in parallel with popular opinions about 'the nature of the beast' and the importance of respectable, middle-class, domestic life. A cat made a home. First, cats were pictured in household scenes, as symbols of comfort and contentment. Then, from around 1800, they were portrayed in an even more sentimental way: with pretty girls, playing with children, in idyllic gardens or dreamlike landscapes. Paintings and photographs of named cats, as individuals, began to appear. Cats had arrived!

Gone – but not forgotten

During the 19th and early 20th centuries, a flood of cloying cat images covered everything from greeting cards and calendars to chocolate boxes. It included troubling images of kittens dressed as children – a sort of 'innocence' overload; however, the hint of cats' supposed inner wickedness had not completely disappeared. Cats remained as a symbol of sin (especially theft or wantonness) in numerous moralising paintings.

Some European painters also deliberately used cats' former reputation to take a walk on the wild side. For example, in *The Artist's Studio* (1855),

Gustave Courbet painted a twisting, turning white cat. Its shape echoes the voluptuous curves of his pale female nude. In *Olympia* (1863), Edouard Manet showed a black cat on his naked model's bed as a sign that she was a prostitute. Both cat and woman share a fierce pride and defiance.

Cats were also favourite subjects for graphic artists such as Swiss-born Théophile Steinlen (1859–1923). One of the best advertising artists the world has ever seen, Steinlen used cats' glowing eyes and sleek silhouettes when designing posters for almost everything – from wholesome cups of tea to shady Paris nightclubs.

And at the same time…

Just like the outrageous artists, some turn-of-the century writers refused be swept along by the sentimental tide of charming kittens:

CAT, n. A soft, indestructible automaton provided by nature to be kicked when things go wrong in the domestic circle.

An entry from *The Devil's Dictionary* (1911) by American writer and satirist Ambrose 'Bitter' Bierce, 1842–1913

Fancy that

It's an odd idea: push dozens of your dearly-loved pets into uncomfortable wire cages, carry them hundreds of miles, and put them on display in a large, noisy, unfamiliar hall, to be gawped at by strangers. Frightened? Panicstricken? If I were a cat, I would be.

Today, breeders taking their pets to cat shows say that their beautiful exhibits don't mind at all. They have been accustomed to the attention since kittenhood; they positively thrive on the admiration they receive. That may very well be true – cats can be adaptable creatures – but, for participants at the very first cat show in Europe, held in 1871 at the Crystal Palace in London, the experience must have been terrifying. It was, however, better than being skinned, trapped or eaten – and all that still happened in Victorian Britain.

Around 170 cats were displayed at that first show. By 1889, similar events were attracting 600 beautiful beasts (or their owners) and over 20,000 visitors. Since then, the Cat Fancy, as enthusiastic cat-breeders are known, has spread worldwide. The first cat show was held in the USA in 1895. In 1906, the American Cat Fancy Association was founded. Today it is 'The World's Largest Registry of Pedigreed Cats'. It classifies purpose-bred cats into four separate types – Natural, Hybrid, Established and Mutant – and recognises 40 current pedigree breeds, plus a few provisionally registered.

Well bred

Abyssinian
American Bobtail
American Curl
American Shorthair
American Wirehair
Balinese
Balinese-Javanese
Birman
Bombay
British Shorthair
Burmese
Burmilla
Chartreux
Chinese Li Hua
Colourpoint Shorthair
Cornish Rex
Devon Rex
Egyptian Mau
European Burmese
Exotic
Havana Brown
Japanese Bobtail

Korat
LaPerm
Maine Coon
Manx
Norwegian Forest Cat
Ocicat
Oriental
Persian
Ragamuffin
Rag Doll
Russian Blue
Scottish Fold
Selkirk Rex
Siamese
Siberian
Singapura
Somali
Sphinx
Tonkinese
Turkish Angora
Turkish Van

A breed too far?

In 1894, American author Mark Twain declared, 'If man could be crossed with the cat, it would improve the man, but it would deteriorate the cat.' From a cat-lover's perspective, that might well be so. But, readers, this writer has a confession: sometimes, this Cat Fancy business seems rather like a feline form of train-spotting. On the other hand, organisations like the AFCA do good and serious work in encouraging breeders to put the welfare of their cats first at all times. However, among unofficial breeds, there are now cats with stumpy legs, miniaturised cats, and many other poor, distorted creatures bred to satisfy human whims and fancies. Even ordinary moggies are beautiful, just as they are. Why mess with nature?

66

I gave an order to a cat, and the cat gave it to its tail.

Chinese proverb

99

CHAPTER NINE

CAT GOT YOUR TONGUE?

From catwalks and catnaps to cats who get the cream, the English language is full of references to cats and their behaviour. So, without rousing a cats' chorus or putting the cat among the pigeons, we should perhaps ask, why? Firstly, people in the past spent a lot of time in cats' company. It could be hard to escape a feline presence in crowded country cottages or city courtyards and alleys. Anyone – everyone – could hardly help noticing cats' distinctive actions. It was a simple step for speakers to start using cats for comparison: a *catlick* for a hasty wash, for example, or a *catseye* for a gleaming precious stone.

Guiding light

In 1934, British engineer Percy Shaw (1889–1975) gave a whole new meaning to the word 'catseye'. He invented a device that has helped millions of motorists and saved countless lives. Shaw's invention was small and simple: a glass stud set into a flexible rubber pad. When fixed to a road surface, the studs reflected light from approaching vehicle headlamps, just like cats' eyes. After dark or in thick fog, they guided drivers in the right direction or warned them of impending hazards.

Percy Shaw's first 50 catseyes were laid at a dangerous road junction: Brightlington Crossroads, near Bradford in Yorkshire. Since then, they have been used to outline road edges, mark the centre of carriageways and at many other potentially dangerous points on busy roads all round the world.

Familiarity with cat behaviour must also have inspired many common sayings, such as:

Curiosity killed the cat.
As deaf as a white cat.
As sick as a cat.
Before the cat can lick its ear. (= never)
Fight like cat and dog.
Like something the cat brought in.
When the cat's away, the mice will play.
There's no cat without claws.

And, from the USA, there is also good ol' country wisdom:

As jumpy as a long-tailed cat in a room full of rocking chairs.

Just like a cat

We also speak of agile, stealthy cat-burglars, loud, wailing catcalls, svelte catsuits and shrieking, scratching catgut violin strings. In fact, strings have never been made from cat intestines; it's sheep who are sacrificed to music-making. But *sheepgut* sounds comfortable, woolly. *Catgut* hints at the raucous, passionate sounds made by cats.

In the same way, common names and phrases may describe cat characteristics or record cruel customs involving cats long ago. Or they may use cats as metaphors, reminding us of the cat's supposedly wild and sinister nature. For example, a cat of nine tails sounds much nastier than a whip with barbed strands. On British ships, until banned in 1948, its sharp spikes drew blood from many a sailor's back like a fierce cat's claws. There are many more:

Let the cat out of the bag (= Disclose a nasty or dangerous or shameful secret.) In the past, at country fairs, unscrupulous dealers offered fattened sucking pigs for sale, tightly tied up in sacks. They warned buyers not to open the sack, in case the 'pig' escaped. Of course, when they did so, back at home, a very cross cat jumped out and ran away.

Bell the cat (= Suggest impossible solutions to a problem.) The story is simple: the mice hold a meeting to discuss how to cope with a marauding cat. 'If we could warn ourselves that he was coming,' one says, 'we could run and hide.' 'Let's hang a bell around his neck,' suggests another mouse, brightly. But how, my friends, but how?

All cats love fish but fear to wet their paws (= We must dare to face danger if we want to achieve our aims.) Shakespeare's Lady Macbeth refers to this traditional saying when she urges Macbeth to commit murder: 'Letting I dare not wait upon I would, like the cat i' the adage.' *Macbeth* act I, scene vii.

Have no room to swing a cat (= Be in a cramped space.) This either refers to the cruel whip mentioned previously, or else, especially in Scotland, means 'no room to hang a rogue'. A further – ghastly – reference is to the barbaric old custom of swinging a cat by its tail as a target for marksmen to shoot at.)

Touch not the cat (= Beware!) Originally the motto of a Highland Scottish clan, Clan Chattan, who honoured mountain wildcats as their totem animals. Their whole motto was 'Touch not the cat but (= unless with) a glove.' It meant: 'Stand back, we're dangerous!'

A cat has nine lives (= A cat is a survivor.) A cat's natural wariness, strength, flexibility and ability to land on its feet certainly do help preserve it from danger, but perhaps there is a little more to this saying than meets the eye. Early versions of it, from the mid-16th century, link cats' survival with women's or witches': 'A woman hath nyne lyves like a cat,' and 'A witch may take on her a cat's body nine times.' But what are we to make of folktales claiming that a cat has 'nine lives, one less than a woman?' Or of Turkish and Arab sayings, that suggest that a cat has seven lives, not nine?

Modern sayings have transformed the nine lives idea yet again: 'A cat has nine lives. For three he plays, for three he strays, and for the last three he stays.'

Raining cats and dogs (= Raining extraordinarily heavily.) Perhaps just a vivid way of describing raindrops that are much, much bigger than usual, but perhaps also a reference to a famous flood caused by a freak storm in London in 1710:

Now in contiguous Drops the Flood comes
  down,
Threat'ning with Deluge this devoted Town...

Now from all Parts the swelling Kennels flow,
And bear their Trophies with them as they go...

Sweeping from Butchers Stalls, Dung, Guts, and
  Blood,
Drown'd Puppies, stinking Sprats, all drench'd
  in Mud,
Dead Cats and Turnip-Tops come tumbling
  down the Flood...

Jonathan Swift, *A Description of a City Shower*, 1710

kennels = gutters

Have kittens! (= Become very agitated or
upset.) This is rather more sinister than it
sounds, and refers to witchcraft. Women who
believed in magic thought that witches could
cast spells to cause terrible pains – like kittens
clawing at the innards. Witches, could, for a
fee or a favour, also cure the problem, by
removing the offending 'kittens' before the
bewitched woman gave birth to them.
Witches' potions could remove unwanted
pregnancies, too; an old slang name for an
abortion was to 'remove a cat from the belly'.

Like a cat on a hot tin roof (= Can't wait, or wild with indiscriminate sexual desire.) The title of a Pulitzer-Prize-winning play by Tennessee Williams, 1955. The Hollywood movie adaptation (1958) was allegedly much disliked by Williams, but did star wildly attractive Paul Newman and smouldering Elizabeth Taylor. Both were nominated for Academy Awards.

And, while sex is still rearing its ugly head…

Cathouse (= Brothel or place where men meet prostitutes.) For centuries, sexually active women, disapproved of by men, have been called 'cats'. This is presumably because a female cat in the mating season attracts a great many would-be partners. Following the same theme, *chasing a cat's tail* was 16th-century slang for womanizing. And as for *pussy*… Even the harmless-sounding *moggie* was originally *maggie*, a rude way of describing a dirty, shabby, untidy old woman. *Grimalkin*, one of Shakespeare's witches' cats, was another name for a prostitute.

Today, the phrase 'like herding cats' usually just means 'a task that is almost impossible', but in the European Middle Ages, 'to lead cats in hell' was a polite expression for sexual frustration.

When we turn to the male of the species, Tom Cat as a nickname for a sexually adventurous man turns out to be only a 20th-century invention. In the Middle Ages, male cats were usually called 'Gibs' (short for Gilbert), or occasionally 'ram-cats'. The popularity of Tom as a name for male cats began in 1760 with the publication of a story-book for children. Titled *The Life and Adventures of a Cat*, it featured a hero-cat called Tom (born poor, found fame and fortune – what else?), and became immensely popular.

At night all cats are grey (= Just don't ask!) An opportunistic, even immoral, expression. If you can't be seen, you won't be caught. So go ahead, regardless. It won't matter.

Who's she – the cat's mother? (= A reproof.) Either 'Be polite and use her proper name!' Or 'She's giving herself airs and graces!'

There are many ways of skinning a cat (= There are many possible ways of solving a problem.) This saying harks back to the times when cats were caught and skinned – sometimes alive – for their fur; in Britain, this ghastly practice fell out of fashion in the 19th century. Today, it is illegal, but, alas, it has not yet completely disappeared. In China and Korea, cats are still farmed for their fur.

A cat may look at a king (= Even the lowest-ranking person can still have an opinion/still has rights.) A celebration of independence and freedom of thought.

See how the cat jumps (= See how things are going to work out, before you join in or give your opinion.) Another saying linking cats to opportunism and self-interest. An implied criticism, comparing cats unfavourably with the devotion of dogs.

At sea, **cats' paws** (= ripples on the surface of water, caused by light breezes) are said to be signs of an approaching storm. This is a link with the old belief that cats and witches can summon up wild winds and waves (page 112).

The Cat and Mouse Act

More properly known as the Prisoners (Temporary Discharge for Ill Health) Act 1913, the 'Cat and Mouse Act' was passed at the height of Suffragette protests in the United Kingdom. Suffragettes were women campaigners who agreed to take direct action – smashing windows, chaining themselves to government buildings, and suchlike – in support of their demands for the right to vote on equal terms with men. After committing acts of minor vandalism, many Suffragette protesters were sent to prison. There, some went on hunger strike, refusing to eat until the government gave in to their demands. Some hunger-strikers were force-fed (an experience they likened to assault, or rape). This caused an outcry among many decent citizens, and so the government passed a new law, which soon became known as the 'Cat and Mouse' Act. It allowed hunger-strikers to be let out of gaol so they could eat and recover their health, but then gave police and prison authorities the power to arrest and detain them all over again, if they dared to continue with their Suffragette protests.

"

As an inspiration to the author I do not think the cat can be over-estimated…His colour and his line alone would serve to give any imaginative creator material for several pages of nervous description…

Carl Van Vechten, *The Tiger in the House*, 1922

"

CHAPTER TEN

CAT CHARACTERS

It had to happen. Just as hip New York artist Andy Warhol (1928–1987) predicted for humans, it seems that every feline will now 'be famous for 15 minutes'. Already there is a website offering advice on how to 'Turn Your Cat into a Social Media Star', together with a list of 'Five Great Cat Twitter Accounts to Follow' (http://www.thedailycat.com/blog/). Indeed, the Internet is (cat-?) littered with creative postings displaying furry pets, in scenarios ranging from cruel to cute and beyond.

A whole catalogue...

However, cats were celebrated long before these newfangled digital displays. There have been brave cats, honoured cats, loved cats, hero cats, working cats, political cats, travelling cats, cats famous for belonging to famous people, and cats that did odd things. Some famous cats are real, some are fictional. So many! Who to choose?

What follows is just a small selection. From it, we can learn – what? That people project their hopes, fears and feelings on to their pets? That imagination is limitless, but life is often stranger? And that some cats really do have remarkable characters?

Explorer cats

A round-the-world voyage was a great and dangerous adventure for a human in 1802–1803, let alone for a feline. The storms, the wild seas, the hunger, the fevers, the changes in climate! But ship's cat **Trim** accompanied British navigator and cartographer Captain Matthew Flinders RN (1774–1814) on this epic journey, and others. He disappeared when Flinders was – most unfairly – kept in gaol in Mauritius for six years. Let Flinders himself write Trim's memorial:

The best and most illustrious of his race,
The most affectionate of friends,
faithful of servants,
and best of creatures
He made the tour of the globe, and a
voyage to Australia,
which he circumnavigated, and was ever
the delight and pleasure of his fellow
voyagers...

Mrs Chippy – in fact, a male – was brought on board Sir Ernest Shackleton's ship *Endurance* by the carpenter (or 'chippy') Harry McNish. Together with the rest of the ship's crew, they set sail in 1914 on the near-fatal Imperial Trans-Antarctic Expedition. Mrs Chippy won the admiration of the crew for his brave, affectionate character, as well as for impressive feats of balance on tilting decks and swaying spars.

In 1915, *Endurance* became trapped in pack-ice and drifted hopelessly. Shackleton claimed that the crew's only chance of survival was to repair and refit a small open boat and make the dangerous sea-crossing to South Georgia, USA. Thanks to McNish's carpentry skills, this was accomplished and they survived, but at tragic cost. Shackleton insisted that Mrs Chippy be shot before the boat set sail. McNish never forgave him.

From heartless sacrifice to something rather ridiculous, stray cat **Casper** (c.1997–2010) could not be kept at home. Every day for over four years, he left his caring owners in Plymouth, south-west England, to wait at the number 3 bus-stop. He then climbed into his favourite seat and made the 11-mile round-trip journey to the city centre and back, while kindly drivers made sure that he did not leave their bus. Few bus journeys are that exciting. So what on earth was in it for Casper? Alas, no-one knows.

Navy cats

For creatures normally so unwilling to submit to regimentation, a surprising number of cats have served on warships – with distinction:

Simon was the ship's cat on Royal Navy ship HMS *Amethyst*. In 1949, the *Amethyst* was fired on by batteries belonging to the Communist People's Liberation Army in China, during their war against nationalists, the Kuomintang. The *Amethyst* was taking no part in the fighting, but suffered severe damage; 22 men died (including the captain), cat Simon was badly hurt. Shocked and shaken by the bombardment, he nevertheless recovered and returned to his duties, killing rats and cheering up the crew. He was promoted to 'Able Seacat Simon' and treated as a celebrity. Sadly, Simon died soon after his ship reached home. But he was awarded the PDSA (People's Dispensary for Sick Animals) Dickin Medal for bravery – the only cat ever to be given this honour.

Oscar the Unsinkable belonged to the German battleship *Bismarck*. His wartime career seems proof that some cats do have several lives. In May 1941 the *Bismarck* was sunk; out of 2,200 crew, only just over 100 were left alive, plus Oscar. The rescue ship, with Oscar on board, was sunk later the same year. Again, Oscar survived. After this, he became the ship's cat of British aircraft carrier, *Ark Royal*. But that splendid ship was also attacked and destroyed; and so, after three near-deaths at sea, the British Navy decided that he was too risky to have on board, and transferred Oscar to a job on shore. Oscar – renamed 'Sam' – retired to a home for sailors in the UK.

Civilian convoy ships and their Navy escorts were some of the most dangerous places to be in World Wars I and II. (There are records of ships' cats refusing to go on board, and ships being sunk a few day's later.)That did not deter **Convoy**, the cat on board British warship HMS *Hermione*. Convoy bravely sailed along with all his shipmates; he was lost with them in 1942, when *Hermione* was sunk by a German torpedo.

Cats' own war

Cats were well known on ships, but the first-recorded airborne hero-cat was **Pyro**, befriended in 1942 by RAF photographer Bob Bird. Named after a chemical used in developing films, Pyro lived on the RAF base at Helensburgh, Scotland. He followed the men as they clambered on board their planes, and seemed to like being in the air. On one flight, at high altitude, he saved Bird from frostbite by warming his frozen fingers. Pyro was posthumously given an award for feline bravery in 2011.

Faith, a female civilian cat, also did her bit for the war effort. In 1936, she strayed into a London church. She was cared for by the priest and parishioners, and regularly attended services. In 1940, at the height of the Blitz bombing raids, Faith gave birth to a kitten and insisted on moving him to the church cellar. Three days later, the church and many nearby buildings were destroyed by a bomb; over 400 people died. But, miraculously, as it seemed, and against all the odds, Faith and her kitten were found alive and well. In the dark days of war, Faith's survival became a symbol of hope for many Londoners.

Space cats

In 1957, animal lovers shed a tear for **Laika**, the dog sent into orbit as part of the USSR space programme. Laika died, from heat and stress, early in her voyage. Fewer people knew, or perhaps cared, that cats also were playing their part in space exploration. For example, in 1963, French 'astrocat' **Félicette** was blasted 100 miles (161 km) into space; electrodes implanted in her brain by scientists monitored her reactions to the shock of the flight. After about 15 minutes, her capsule floated back down to earth. Félicette survived, although other space cats were less fortunate.

Political Cats

Cats feature in the life stories of so many political leaders, from London Lord Mayor Dick Whittington (died 1423) to US President Bill Clinton, owner of the redoubtable and seemingly media-savvy cat

Socks. In real life, Whittington probably did not have a cat, nor did he rise from dire poverty to great riches (both details were added to his biography by later writers) – but, as politicians and their advisors have known throughout the ages, it can be a mistake to let the facts get in the way of a good story. UK prime minister Winston Churchill was genuinely fond of cats – and rarely missed an opportunity to be photographed with one.

Rather less happy news-management issues swirled around **Humphrey**, the cat who joined the staff of the British prime minister's residence as a much-needed mouse-catcher in 1988. He was accused of munching his way through a nestful of baby robins, and the prime minister himself had to issue a denial. Later, dark rumours about Humphrey's alleged untimely end at the hands of a new government were circulated by its opponents. They proved false, although Humphrey had 'enjoyed' a rather rapid retirement.

Until recently, civil servants in old buildings still paid for cats to control rodents (they were cheaper than human pest destroyers). So did libraries and museums. In Scotland, **Smudge** (1979–1999), the cat at the People's Palace museum in Glasgow, hit the headlines when it was recruited as a member of a trades union. However, according to the *Guinness Book of Records*, the world's best mouser was **Towser**, the cat employed at Glenturret Whisky Distillery in Scotland. In a long career of over 20 years, he was reckoned to have accounted for almost 30,000 victims.

Other government departments employed cats in different ways. In 2006, for example, **Fred the Undercover Kitty** helped New York Police Department to arrest a man accused of rather an unusual crime: impersonating a veterinary surgeon.

Yes, really…

Some cats achieve fame by their own efforts, however bizarrely. Others have notoriety thrust upon them. In 1984, Grey Manx cat **All Ball** was chosen to be the pet of Koko (born 1971), a tame gorilla in California, USA. In 2005, **Red** received a bequest of 1.3 million

Canadian dollars from a shy, reclusive gardener. In 2009, US cat **Nora** featured as soloist in the first performance of CATcerto, a work for piano and orchestra by Lithuanian composer Mindaugas Piecaitis. In 2002, **CC (Carbon Copy)** won fame and excited horror fans by becoming the first cloned kitten ever born, in Texas, USA; in 2008, newspaper readers were alarmed by reports of Chinese cats apparently growing wings.*

Almost 3,500 years earlier, something (love? loss? pride in ownership?) prompted an ancient Egyptian government scribe to record the death of his cat, **Nadjem** (Sweetie) – making his pet the first-known named cat on the planet. In 2012, a serious British newspaper claimed that cat **Orlando** outdid financial experts in the choice of its investments; it apparently chose the 'best' shares by patting a toy mouse around a numbered board.**

*http://www.telegraph.co.uk/news/newstopics/howaboutthat/2631016/Chinese-cats-grow-wings.html

** http://www.guardian.co.uk/money/2012/apr/07/ftse-share-picking-challenge-cat

Cat fantasy

All these cats were real, but what about imaginary cat characters? Many of them are even more famous than living and breathing moggies. The father of them all must be **Puss in Boots**, first described in writing by French author Charles Perrault (1628–1703) but possibly based on much older folktales. It's a very ambiguous story: Puss is clever and resourceful but deeply dishonest. One 19th-century reader called it 'a lesson in lying', but it's still one of the most popular plots for Christmas pantomimes. Then there's Lewis Carroll's grinning, vanishing **Cheshire Cat** (1865) from *Alice's Adventures in Wonderland*; and there's Edward Lear's nonsense *The Owl and Pussycat* (1871), which was celebrated in 2012 by an International Owl and Pussycat Day (!).

For lovers of horror-fiction there's the classic chiller short-story *The Black Cat* (1843) by US author Edgar Allen Poe. At the other end of the fictional scale, we can read Beatrix Potter's humanised *Tom Kitten*, published in 1907 in the UK, very much for children. Or there's **Orlando** the magnificent marmalade cat, hero of 19 volumes (1938–1972) by Kathleen Hale– a breath of fresh air, with witty plots, as well as big and beautiful book design. From the USA, there's Dr Seuss's scatty *The Cat in the Hat* (1957), a fun way to learn reading. There are fast-paced, violent Hollywood *Tom and Jerry* films (1940 and still going) and big fat lazy cartoon cat *Garfield* (1978), a ginger blob with a passion for lasagne. On US children's TV, since 2001, *Sagwa*, a pretty Chinese cat, has skipped across the screen, teaching moral 'life lessons'.

And there's T.S. Eliot's *Old Possum's Book of Practical Cats* (1939). Often described as 'whimsical', you either love or hate these poems. Today they are best known for inspiring the wildly successful *CATS* musical, composed by Andrew Lloyd-Webber. First performed in 1981, with dramatic choreography and lifelike cat costumes, it broke records (now overtaken) as the longest-running musical in British stage history; its lyrics have been translated into over 20 languages.

Cat fantastic

Last but not least, in Japan we find two famous cat characters that cross all the boundaries between real and imaginary:

Maneki Neko (beckoning cat) is the little painted ceramic white-and-tortoiseshell cat figurine that stands at the entrance to Japanese shops and bars. It has one paw, or occasionally two, raised above its head in a traditional beckoning gesture. Sometimes it holds a gold coin, a symbol of wealth.

Maneki Neko is said to be a traditional lucky charm, attracting money, good fortune and friends. However, there is no record of it anywhere before around 1870, and its origins are uncertain. That has not, however, prevented various 'new' legends growing up to give Maneki Neko a back-story. Perhaps it was first presented to an old woman robbed of her pet, or to a young woman whose cat was murdered by a jealous suitor? Or perhaps it commemorates a spirit cat who saved the life of a nobleman by leading him away from enemies waiting to ambush him?

Hello Kitty is something similar – and completely different. She is a little, girly, character, with cat ears and a big red bow in her hair. She was created in 1974 for the Japanese Sanrio Corporation. Somewhat strangely, she herself has a pet cat, 'Charmmy Kitty'.

Originally designed as a decorative motif to add value to gift merchandise directed at pre-teenage girls, by the 1990s Hello Kitty had become a global phenomenon. Goods decorated with her image sold to adults as well as children, men as well as women; the Hello Kitty brand had its own TV shows, books, computer games, theme-parks, wines, watches, jewellery and clothes. There was even a passenger jet plane decorated with the Hello Kitty logo. In the mid 2000s the brand was earning around half a billion US dollars every year. Hello Kitty appealed because she was the essence of the fashionable *kawaii* (cute, whimsical, youthful, submissive) style in Japanese culture. But she is – even more than other cat characters – a child, not a feline.

Cat cafés

In Japan, if you choose, you can visit one of around 150 'cat cafés'. No, not to eat cat-meat (though, alas, that can still be done in some places, including China and Korea). Instead, cat cafes exist to meet a need. Customers go to cafés to experience cat company. Each café is equipped (if that is the word) with from 12 to 24 friendly furries, trained to accept the caresses of complete strangers for an hour or two. Their human visitors – or clients – may be seeking sensory pleasure, undemanding animal friendship or possibly some kind of therapeutic companionship with a living creature that does not judge, reject, criticise, compare or complain. Almost certainly, the humans benefit from the experience. Many studies have shown that stroking a cat or listening to its purr can relieve stress, calm frantic heartbeats and lower blood pressure. The pleasure of a warm, friendly welcome is harder to quantify, but almost certainly just as valuable.

Cats have their uses…

What are we to learn from the cat-café phenomenon? In fact, what can we learn from the centuries-old, worldwide custom of first tolerating cats around the home or farm, and then, enthusiastically, keeping cats as pets? Certainly, that cats are useful – for their fur, their meat, and as fertilisers. (One gentle clergyman, famous for his beautiful rose-garden, was rumoured to bury a dead cat under every bush.) Cats have a proven record as pest-controllers, and, in times of fuel poverty, have even been used for keeping warm. American poet Sylvia Plath told how, when visiting a grand and chilly English home one winter, her hostess offered guests the choice between a cat and a hot-water bottle. Whether feared and loathed or liked and admired, cats have been used as symbols of grace or of supernatural evil, and have served as an inspiration for artists of all kinds.

In danger – and dangerous

Clearly, cats are tough, self-sufficient survivors – although today, the pure native Scottish wildcat, *Felis sylvestris grampia*, is rarer than the tiger, thanks to interbreeding with farm cats and gamekeeper persecution. In many big cities, colonies of feral cats cause concern (how can they be fed?) and controversy (would euthanasia be better for them than a life of semi-starvation?).

Undoubtedly, cats have caused extreme environmental damage. They have been implicated in the extinction of several local species, such as *hutia* (large guinea-pig-like mammals) in the Caribbean region, and, most famously, the Stephens Island wren (New Zealand) – which was wiped out by imported cats in just a few years, soon after 1894. To save local seabirds, all felines were forcibly removed from Ascension Island in the South Atlantic in 2004. Similar cat-eradication schemes are underway in many other places.

Pet cats kill an unknown number of wild birds, small mammals, insects, frogs and lizards. In 2012, American scientists fitted cats with miniature cameras to record their hunting activities. They found that, while only one cat in three is an effective predator, cats that do hunt kill on average two creatures per week – and are responsible for the decline in around one-third of native American garden birds. And, last but by no means least, according to the *New York Times*, in 2009, the petfood industry was consuming around 10 per cent of the world's available forage fish. At a time when the world's oceans are often said to be in crisis, can this really be justified?

Playing and learning

Cats have long been valued as playthings for children, or as living objects that we may 'learn benevolence upon'. In the past, they performed tricks in 'cat circuses'; today, they feature in advertisements and films, and at least one travelling 'acrobatic cat' show survives in the USA. For many years, cats have been the subjects of scientific experiments – some sounding very horrible. A (thankfully hypothetical) dead cat remains the subject of a famous scientific and mathematical conundrum: the quantum physics paradox of Schrödinger's cat, first formulated in 1935. And what are we to make of the genetically modified cats that glow green in the dark? Developed in 2011, the green glow (from jellyfish) is used to mark the presence of further genes introduced from another species (monkeys) that appear to help protect living creatures from AIDS. Scientists hope that by studying the marked cells in cats, they may help save human lives.

All you need is (cat) love?

Many cat-lovers would sympathise with the plight of the owners of Oscar, a cat who lost his back legs in 2010 while dozing in the path of a combine harvester. But few would ask to have their pet fitted with the world's first 'bionic' cat limbs by one of Britain's leading biomedical engineers. In fact, Oscar's artificial legs are helping to solve problems faced by humans who have lost limbs – and Oscar himself is well and happy and can move around normally. Probably even fewer would want to imitate the 60-year-old woman in Sweden who was found, also in 2010, to be living with her mother, her sister, her son and no less than 191 domestic moggies. Swedish social services acted fast, as soon as the house full of cats – and the stench of ammonia from cat urine – was discovered. They took most of the cats away to be destroyed, saying that they were sick or injured, and reminded everyone that, in Sweden, keeping more than nine cats is strictly illegal.

However, the world's ultimate cat-lover must be the the German postman who, in 2010, unofficially 'married' his dying cat. He hired an actress to impersonate the registrar at the ceremony, saying that he and his cat, Cecilia, had spent 10 very happy years together and so getting married, before Cecilia died, was what he really wanted to do.

Yes! Cats are contradictory. If we describe them in value-laden, human terms, they are beautiful and destructive, soft, gentle, heartless and cruel. Yet cats, like people, can be loveable, loved, and loving. They are nothing like us, and yet they show us to ourselves.

Glossary

ancestors Earlier generations of a human or animal family: parents, grandparents, great-grandparents and so on.

archaeologists People who study the physical remains of the past.

auspicious Bringing good fortune.

barometric pressure The pressure of the atmosphere on the earth. High pressure is often a sign of fine weather, low pressure a sign of storms.

binocular vision Using two eyes together. This makes it easier to see faint objects and to judge depth and distance.

carnassials Curved teeth in a cat's upper and lower jaw, towards the back of the mouth. They act like shears to cut meat.

carnivore Meat-eating animal; an **obligate carnivore** is an animal that can only survive on a meat-based diet.

catnip A herb. When eaten or inhaled, it causes pleasurable sensations for some cats.

cerebellum Area of the brain that controls balance.

circulatory system The heart and the network of veins, arteries and capillaries that allow blood to flow round the body. Blood carries fresh oxygen from the lungs to body cells, together with other essential substances.

civet (1) A musky, strong-smelling substance from glands near a civet's (2) tail. Until the 20th century, used in perfumery.

civet (2) Small catlike animal: the best-known species is *Civettictis civetta*.

descendants People or animals born to the same parents, grandparents, great-grandparents and so on.

deter Discourage, prevent.

diabolical Like a devil.

dilate Open wide.

diminutive Very small.

disorientated Confused; not knowing position or direction.

distal end The far end of something, e.g. a fingertip.

domestic Belonging to a house or home.

dominant Most powerful.

electromagnetic waves A form of energy, radiated (sent out) as waves. Radio waves, microwaves, visible light and X-rays are all different kinds of electromagnetic waves.

excretion The processes of getting rid of waste from the body.

exemplar Example to be copied.

faeces Waste excreted from the body after digestion.

familiars According to past beliefs, evil spirits that took the form of cats and other small animals and visited witches.

field of view The area visible through a camera lens or from a living creature's eyes.

Flehmen reaction Cat behaviour (wide-open mouth, flick of tongue) when sensing faint smells.

focal length The distance between a lens in a cat's eye and the point where rays of light passing through it come to a focus (sharp clear image) on the retina.

gene A molecule (collection of atoms) that holds the

information needed to build and maintain the cells of a living animal (or plant) and passes that information on to the next generation.

geologists People who study rocks and fossils.

hallucinogenic A substance that disturbs the brain, causing dreamlike or nightmare sensations.

heretic Someone who disobeys or argues against the teachings of the Christian Church.

idyllic Extremely pleasant, beautiful and peaceful.

incisors Small, sharp teeth at the front of a mammal's mouth.

ingest Take into the body, for example by eating or sniffing.

KT Horizon (or KT Boundary) The name given by geologists to a thin layer of rock around 65 million years old. It was laid down around the time that the dinosaurs became extinct. Scientists use it to mark the boundary between the Cretaceous and Tertiary geological time-periods.

land bridge Area of dry sea-bed between two land masses left uncovered during past Ice Ages, when seas and oceans froze.

ligaments Strong, stretchy bands of living tissue that attach bones to bones.

mammal A living creature that suckles its young. Cats (and humans) are mammals.

marsupial Animal that rears its young in a pouch, e.g. a kangaroo.

metabolise Break down food inside the body to obtain energy plus substances essential for life, such as vitamins and minerals.

metaphor A way of speaking or writing when one object is compared with something completely different. Often used by poets or in popular sayings, for example: 'It's raining cats and dogs.'

molecule A collection of atoms linked together in a particular combination to make a substance. For example, a water molecule is made of hydrogen and oxygen atoms.

mused Thought deeply about.

Nirvana According to Hindu, Buddhist and other Asian religious beliefs, the time when a soul finds everlasting peace after death.

occult Hidden and sinister.

olfactory receptors Special cells that are sensitive to scent molecules.

pagan Religious beliefs held by people before the spread of Judaism, Christianity and Islam.

pageant Procession, usually in costume and with music, to celebrate an important past event.

perianal glands Parts of the body (beneath a cat's or a civet's tail) that produce a very strong-smelling substance.

pinna Outer flap of a cat's ear.

plague A life-threatening infection caused by bacteria. Often spread by bites from infected fleas. Symptoms include fever and large black swellings.

polydactyly Having more than the usual number of fingers or toes.

posthumously After death.

promiscuous With many different partners.

pupil Black area at the centre of the eye. In cats, it can change from a narrow slit to a wide circle.

rabies A deadly disease, caused by a virus. It attacks the brain. Can be spread by bites from infected mammals.

rational Reasonable, logical.

retina Layer of light-sensitive cells at the back of the cat's eye.

retractable Able to be pulled back or pulled in.

retracted Pulled back or pulled in.

righting reflex A series of movements performed by a cat when it senses that it is upside down and falling. These place it in the safest possible position for landing. They are involuntary (performed automatically): the cat does not have to think about them.

rodents Animals, for example rats and mice, with long sharp incisors (front teeth) used to nibble and gnaw food.

spars Long, strong poles used on board sailing ships, for example, as masts or yards (poles from which sails were hung).

species A group of living creatures that share the same characteristics and can (usually) breed together, although they may not do so. The lowest rank of the system of classification and naming used by scientists: Life > domain > kingdom > phylum > class > order > family > genus > species.

subspecies Separate group within a species. Animals' scientific names show their genus, species and (sometimes) subspecies. The domestic cat is *Felis* (genus), *sylvaticus* (species) *catus* (subspecies).

tableaux In the past, a form of street theatre. Actors
and musicians dressed in costume presented 'living
pictures' of important events.

tapetum lucidum The mirror-like panel behind the
retina in a cat's eye. It reflects light back to the retina
and helps cats see in the dark.

tendons Tough, stretchy bands of living tissue that
connect muscles to bones.

toxoplasmosis A disease caused by a microscopic
parasite. It is spread by contact with uncooked meat
or by animal faeces, especially that of cats.

unrequited Unfulfilled.

vomeronasal organ Sensor at the back of a cat's
mouth that can detect very faint smells.

vermin Pests.

vertebrae Bones that make up the spine (backbone) of
cats and many other animals.

voluptuous Full, generous, shapely, luxurious.

Cats timeline

c.65,000,000 BC The Miacids, remote ancestors of the cat family, live on earth.

c.53,000,000 BC The Feloidea (also known as Feliformia) evolve from the Miacids. They become the ancestors of many later catlike species.

c.30,000,000 BC *Proailurus* evolves from the Feloidea. It has retractable claws.

c.20,000,000 BC *Sivaelurus* evolves from *Proailurus*.

c.18,000,000 BC Felidae, the first true cats, evolve from *Sivaelurus*.

c.12,000,000 BC *Felis*, the earliest small cats, evolve from the Felidae.

c.2,000,000 BC Wildcat species (*Felis sylvestris*), distant ancestor of the domestic cat, evolves from *Felis*.

c.153,000–105,000 BC 'First Five Females' (all members of subspecies *Felis sylvestris lybica*) live in the Near East. All modern domestic cats are descended from them.

c.9,000 BC Farmers build earliest villages, in the Near East. Cats choose to go and live with them.

c.7,500 BC People on Cyprus bury a pet or prized cat alongside an important dead person.

c.3,600 BC Cats are portrayed in ancient Egyptian wall paintings.

c.2000 BC Cats spread east to Turkey and into Asia.

c.1500 BC More ancient Egyptians begin to keep cats, perhaps to guard grainstores, perhaps as pets.

c.900 BC Phoenician traders transport cats to lands around the Mediterranean Sea, and perhaps as far as the south-west British Isles.

c.800–300 BC Pet cats are recorded in ancient Greece. Cats are said to be sacred to Diana, goddess of hunting.

c.700 BC–AD 400 Among Celtic tribes in Europe, cats are thought to have magic powers. They are sacred to the Moon. They are sometimes sacrificed to foretell the future.

c.660 BC Worship of cat-goddess Bubastis becomes popular in Egypt. Many thousands of mummified cats are offered to her, at temples.

c.450 BC Greek traveller and historian Herodotus reports severe punishments for killing cats in Egypt.

c.400 BC–AD 400 Pets cats are known in Ancient Rome, but are not common. They also live on board ships and on farms. For soldiers, they are symbols of fierceness. Cats are said to be sacred to Libertas, goddess of freedom.

c.200 BC–AD 400 Cats reach China and spread through south-east Asia.

c.AD 400–1700 Some old Celtic beliefs and rituals involving cats continue in north and west Europe. However, cats are also trapped and killed for their fur.

c. 600 Cats reach Japan.

c. 630 The Prophet Muhammad and the Holy Qur'an encourage people in Muslim lands to respect living creatures, including cats.

c. 800 Anonymous Irish monk writes poem about cat Pangur Ban.

c.800–1100 To the Vikings, cats are symbols of fertility, and sacred to Freyja, goddess of love. They are also trapped for their fur.

942 In Wales, King Hywel Dda passes law to protect farm cats.

c.1000–1700 Christian leaders in Europe associate cats with ancient pagan practices and witchcraft.

c.1345–1700 Cats, suspected as carriers of plague in many parts of Europe, are hunted and killed. They are used for target practice, burned on bonfires, and mistreated in 'folkloric games'.

c.1350–1767 *The Cat-Book Poems*, admiring cats' beauty, are written and illustrated in Siam (now Thailand).

c.1400–1700 Cats are accused of being 'familiars' (evil spirits). Cats are also bricked up in walls and under threshholds, to keep evil spirits away.

c.1450 European artists begin to study cats for their shape and grace.

c.1560 French philosopher Michel de Montaigne is one of the first to suggest that cats have the power to think.

c.1600–1800 Cats are used to make sounds in 'cat organs'.

c.1600 Exotic cats – e.g. long-haired Angoras, from Turkey – are first seen in Europe. They are much admired.

1605 English clergyman Edward Topsell publishes translation of *Historia Animalium*, one of the first books to suggest that cats can feel love for their owners.

1605 Around this time, a cat is added to the popular story of Dick Whittington, medieval Lord Mayor of London.

c.1606 Dramatist William Shakespeare links cats with witches in his play *Macbeth*.

1637 French philosopher and mathematician René Descartes repeats the old belief that animals do not feel pain.

1650 Story – perhaps not true – of the 'Kilkenny cats' (see page 91).

c.1700–1800 Pet cats are often mentioned in books, poems, diaries, letters.

1727 French author Moncrif publishes the first book in Europe entirely about cats.

c.1730 The Great Cat Massacre in Paris. Rough, hungry, poorly-paid apprentices torture and hang cats as a protest against their low wages and miserable living conditions. They claim that the cats are better cared for than they are, and know that their action will cause their wealthy employer to suffer anguish; the cats are his wife's pets. By the 1730s, people with money to spare and a 'polite' education have become pet-lovers; poor, uneducated working people have not.

1747–1788 French naturalist Buffon publishes detailed scientific drawings of different cat breeds.

1789 British philosopher Jeremy Bentham calls for laws to treat animals well.

1794 Naturalist Erasmus Darwin reports that animals have feelings of friendship, for each other and for humans.

c.1800–1900 Remains of cat mummies shipped from Egypt to Europe, to be used as fertiliser.

1843 American author Edgar Allen Poe writes horror story, *The Black Cat*.

CATS: A VERY PECULIAR HISTORY

c.1850–1950 Sentimental images of cats become very popular, as decorations and in mass media. Images of cats are also used, to shock, by controversial artists, and to create striking advertising posters.

1865 British author Lewis Carroll creates the strange Cheshire Cat in his book *The Adventures of Alice in Wonderland*.

1871 British artist and poet Edward Lear writes *The Owl and the Pussycat*.

1871 First cat show in Europe, held in London.

1895 First cat show in USA.

1906 American Cat Fancy Association founded.

1907 British artist Beatrix Potter paints (and writes about) *Tom Kitten*.

1913 'Cat and Mouse Act' (used to imprison Suffragette protestors) passed by British parliament.

1934 British engineer Percy Shaw invents 'cat's eyes' road safety markings.

1939 American-British poet T.S. Eliot writes *Old Possum's Book of Practical Cats*.

1940 First Hollywood cartoon film featuring cat Tom and mouse Jerry.

1949 UK navy cat Simon survives attack on his ship; he is later awarded the prestigious Dickin Medal for brave animals.

1857 American author Dr Seuss publishes reading book *The Cat in the Hat*.

1963 French scientists send cat Félicette on a flight to test space rockets.

1974 Merchandising character Hello Kitty created in Japan.

1978 Cartoon cat Garfield first appears in print.

1981 *CATS*, the musical by Andrew Lloyd Webber, is first performed.

1988 Humphrey the cat goes to live in UK prime minister's residence in London.

1998 Natural civet extract banned from perfumery in Europe.

2002 First cloned kitten, CC, born in USA.

2004 Archaeologists discover remains of pet or prized cat, buried c.7500 BC in Cyprus.

2007 Geneticists discover 'First Five Female' ancestors of all domestic cats.

2011 Royal Air Force cat Pyro posthumously given bravery award.

2012 Cat in Boston, USA, reported to have survived a fall of around 60 metres (200 feet).

2012 Japanese scientists show that cats use electromagnetic radiation to sense approaching earthquakes.

Index